The Criminal Lawyer's Job

A Survival Guide

Amber L. St. Clair

Series created and edited by International Legal Publishers, LLC

Real Lawyering
Books That Make Lawyers' Jobs Easier

GP | Solo
ABA General Practice, Solo & Small Firm Division

Cover design by ABA Publishing.

The materials contained herein represent the opinions and views of the authors and/or the editors, and should not be construed to be the views or opinions of the law firms or companies with whom such persons are in partnership with, associated with, or employed by, nor of the American Bar Association or the General Practice, Solo and Small Firm Section, unless adopted pursuant to the bylaws of the Association.

Nothing contained in this book is to be considered as the rendering of legal advice, either generally or in connection with any specific issue or case; nor do these materials purport to explain or interpret any specific bond or policy, or any provisions thereof, issued by any particular franchise company, or to render franchise or other professional advice. Readers are responsible for obtaining advice from their own lawyers or other professionals. This book and any forms and agreements herein are intended for educational and informational purposes only.

Printed in the United States of America

Library of Congress Cataloging-in-Publication Data

St. Clair, Amber L., 1970-
    The criminal lawyer's job : a survival guide / by Amber L. St. Clair.
       p. cm.
    Includes index.
    ISBN 1-59031-694-0
    1. Defense (Criminal procedure)—United States. 2. Trial practice—United States.
I. Title.

KF9656.S7 2006
345.73'05044—dc22

                                                                                          2006023913

Discounts are available for books ordered in bulk. Special consideration is given to state bars, CLE programs, and other bar-related organizations. Inquire at Book Publishing, ABA Publishing, American Bar Association, 321 North Clark Street, Chicago, Illinois 60610-4714.

www.ababooks.org

Contents

Foreword

I will *assume* you have purchased this book because you have been recently retained by an individual who is alleged to have done something criminal (or at least minimally naughty). Perhaps you have never represented such an individual or do not fancy yourself an experienced criminal defense attorney. Consider this guide a hand to hold along the journey through the criminal justice system.

You can use the techniques I discuss in this book to assist you in defending clients with pending traffic tickets, petty offenses, misdemeanors, and felonies. Its principles can be applied in administrative law court, municipal court, state court, and federal court—any court and jurisdiction in which your client is charged with a violation of the law. Although most of my examples focus on defending clients charged with blue-collar felonies in state court, these techniques can be used to defend clients charged with misdemeanors or white-collar crimes as well.

This book will not make you Perry Mason, nor will it give you directions to the courthouse. It will not teach you how to find clients or how to bill them. Instead, it is intended as a guide for new criminal defense lawyers and for some old fogies who have lost their way. It will walk you from point A (the initial client meeting) to point Z (picking a jury and trying a case). This guide is NOT intended to be a summary of the law or an expert opinion regarding the practice of criminal law. It does not deal with post-trial or juvenile matters—those areas of law require their own separate treatises. It is a cheat sheet, if you will; it is a guide most senior criminal defense attorneys will wish they had when they started practicing, although most will never admit it.

About the Author

Amber L. St. Clair has an extensive background in criminal trials and civil lawsuits. Ms. St. Clair has been a criminal defense lawyer for many years and began her career as a prosecutor. In addition, she has extensive litigation experience in the areas of medical and professional liability, personal injury, and products liability. Recognized for excellence by her peers, Ms. St. Clair has tried more than 100 trials, having received "not guilty" verdicts in cases involving murder, kidnapping, rape, sex crimes, robbery, drugs, assault, battery, arson, and DUI, among others. Her jury trial win percentage is far above the national average. Her trial skills were featured live on Court TV, where she received glowing reviews from the commentators and the majority of the viewing public's support. Ms. St. Clair is licensed to practice in Colorado and Kansas. She presently manages her own law firm in Golden, Colorado, where she handles primarily felony criminal defense matters.

Ms. St. Clair graduated with honors from Washburn University School of Law. While in law school, she was inducted into the Order of the Barristers; admitted to both the Moot Court and Trial Advocacy teams; awarded top paper in Products Liability class, the CALI Excellence Award for Excellent Achievement in the Study of Products Liability, and top speaker in the Washburn Intramural Trial Advocacy Competition; recognized for the Washburn University Moot Court Counsel Outstanding Student Brief; nominated to Who's Who Among American Universities and Colleges; invited to join the local American Inn of Court; and given one of two student positions on the law school admissions board. She also achieved various feats in both the national moot court and trial advocacy arenas. Ms. St. Clair graduated magna cum laude from Baker University with a Bachelor of Arts degree in history, political science, and philosophy.

CHAPTER 1

General Overview of the Criminal Justice Process

There are approximately 18 stages to the criminal justice process, give or take a few depending upon your jurisdiction's procedural rules.

1. CRIME IS ALLEGED TO HAVE OCCURRED

The criminal justice process begins when someone makes an allegation that a crime has occurred. The allegation can be made by a law enforcement officer (sometimes they are the only witness to a crime, e.g., a traffic law violation) or a private citizen. At this point, your prospective client is known as the suspect.

2. POLICE CONDUCT AN INVESTIGATION

Once a crime is alleged, law enforcement officers will begin to investigate. The complaining witness or aggrieved victim will make a statement and written reports will be made of these statements. If the only witness involves law enforcement, the officers will make written reports documenting what they observed.

If the investigating officer determines that there are other witnesses to the crime, she may take statements from these people.

Evidence, if any, will be gathered at this time by collecting physical evidence located at the crime scene, taking photographs and video images of the scene and evidence, and retrieving relevant evidence from other locations.

Crime scene analysts may be asked to test various pieces of evidence or conduct examinations that may reveal further evidence (e.g., fingerprint analysis, chemical analysis of various substances).

The suspect (who will later become the defendant and your client) will be questioned at this time by the investigating officer. Note: You will probably

1

not be involved at this stage. Most defendants do not know any lawyers or do not have the money to pay a lawyer for advice before speaking to the police. Law enforcement officers must advise him of his rights if he is questioned in a custodial setting. But the client is usually on his own at this point when choosing to waive his rights and speak with investigators.

A search warrant is necessary if the evidence is not in plain view or officers have no consent from the owner to search the thing that may contain the additional evidence. A search warrant is obtained if an investigating officer believes that there is additional evidence to the alleged crime somewhere else.

3. ARREST IS MADE

If sufficient grounds exist, the suspect will be taken into custody to be booked (have his prints and his mug shot taken) and may be charged.

4. CRIME IS CHARGED

If sufficient grounds exist, the suspect may be charged with a crime or violation of the law. All alleged violations of the law are set out in a charging document. This document seeks to notify the accused of the charge and the law he is alleged to have violated. The defense attorney is not involved in drafting or negotiating this document.

As you may remember from your criminal procedure class, a charge can be brought in several ways.

Investigating Officer

Traffic infractions, petty offenses, and misdemeanor crimes can be charged by the investigating law enforcement officer at the time of the initial contact with the suspect. The officer can prepare the charging document herself. Ordinarily there is a uniform charging document or form used by the officer. A carbon copy is served upon the defendant at the time. A speeding ticket is an example of such a charging document. These charging documents notify the defendant of the time and place to appear in court to answer to the charges. If the officer works for a municipality, the charging document will direct the defendant to appear in municipal court. If the officer works for the sheriff's department or state patrol, the charging document will likely direct the defendant to appear in district court. If the suspect is not taken into custody, he is free to leave.

Grand Jury Indictment

A crime can also be charged by a grand jury. In this instance, the prosecuting attorney conducts her own investigation into allegations of a crime. A grand jury is convened pursuant to the jurisdiction's law, and the prosecutor presents testimony and evidence to the grand jury. The court's permission is not required to convene a grand jury, and the court is not involved unless the prosecutor requests the court to compel a witness to testify.

The prosecutor asks questions of the various witnesses subpoenaed to testify before the grand jury and introduces exhibits through their testimony. Sometimes the members of the jury ask questions.

After all the evidence is presented, the prosecutor asks the grand jury to take a vote and indict on various charges submitted to the grand jury by the prosecutor. If the grand jury indicts, its finding will be formalized into a written indictment that acts as the charging document. This indictment consists of a plain and concise statement of the essential facts constituting the crime charged. It notifies the defendant of the crime with which he is charged and the sections of the law he is alleged to have violated. It is signed by the grand jury foreman.

Often, defendants are not made aware of these proceedings. There is no right to have counsel appear on defendant's behalf.

Complaint and Information

If the crime alleged is more serious than a traffic offense, petty offense, or certain low-level misdemeanors, it will be presented by the lead investigating office to the jurisdiction's prosecuting attorney. The prosecutor will review the facts and circumstances surrounding the alleged crime and make a determination as to whether a crime will be charged and at what severity level. If the crime is not a felony, a summons or notice to appear may be issued to the defendant along with a Complaint and Information notifying the defendant of the crime with which he is charged, the sections of the law he is alleged to have violated, and the time and place to appear to answer to the charges.

Some jurisdictions separate the Complaint and Information in felony cases. The Complaint is filed first to commence the prosecution. It includes the crime charged and sections of the law alleged to have been violated. The Information is filed after the preliminary hearing. It includes a plain and concise statement of the essential facts constituting the crime charged.

A sample Complaint and Information/Felony is included as Exhibit A, and a sample Complaint/Misdemeanor is included as Exhibit B on the enclosed CD-ROM. ●➤

Affidavit of Probable Cause

If the charge includes a felony, in addition to the complaint and information the prosecutor will prepare an affidavit of probable cause that will be sworn to by the lead investigating officer. It usually consists of a summary of all the investigating officers' reports. It alleges facts to support probable cause to believe a felony has been committed and probable cause to believe the defendant has committed the felony. It requests the court to order the defendant to be brought to court to answer the charges. Depending upon the severity level of the crime, the affidavit may request an arrest warrant. Thereafter, the warrant will be executed by the court and the defendant will be brought to court to answer the charges. The defendant will be required to post bail or provide a bond in order to get out of custody.

If the charges are less severe (e.g., it is not a crime of violence, or it is a crime that does not carry a significant prison sentence), the affidavit may request that the defendant be summoned to court. That means that he can appear on his own without the need for arrest or to post bail.

5. ADVISEMENT OF THE CHARGE

The first time the defendant appears in front of the judge in a felony case is often called the Advisement. In a misdemeanor case, this first appearance is often called the Arraignment.

If defendant has posted bail or has been ordered to appear on summons, he will appear in a courtroom at a designated time and place. The court advises the defendant of the charges against him, certain constitutional rights, and, if he is still in custody, the amount of bail. Thereafter, the matter may be continued to another date for an attorney to appear with the defendant.

6. DEFENDANT CONTACTS ATTORNEY REGARDING REPRESENTATION

Usually at this point, the defendant (or someone on his behalf) contacts you regarding representation.

Most clients will seek your help after they have been charged. Most often, they are not financially able to seek your help before a matter is charged. Usually only affluent clients, those being investigated for white-collar crimes, and those who know they are being investigated by a grand jury will enlist the services of an attorney before the matter is charged. (Precharge representation is not covered in this book.)

7. CLIENT RETAINS YOUR SERVICES

If you agree to take the case, you are "retained." Smart lawyers always get their fees paid in advance. If necessary to assist you in requiring your fee paid in advance, buy or rent a credit card machine. A wise attorney once told me, "Always get your money up front and never expect to make anything more than what you get up front." Regardless of when you obtain your fee, you should sign a retainer agreement with the client outlining the parameters of your representation.

8. MEETING WITH THE CLIENT FACE-TO-FACE

Meet with the client before filing any motion or entering your appearance (defined below). During this meeting, you will

▶   Review the charges with the defendant.

▶   Review the evidence required to establish the charges.

▶   Review the potential penalties and other consequences.

▶   Review the discovery you have obtained, if you have any.

▶   Review the attorney–client privilege.

▶   Review various expectations you have of the client.

▶   Determine how the client would like to proceed.

▶   Describe the process and proceedings yet to come, including the antici-pated timeline.

▶   Obtain the client's pertinent background information.

9. FIRST APPEARANCE

Courts in most jurisdictions will set a First Appearance or Advisement in order to give the defendant an opportunity to appear with an attorney and schedule future proceedings such as a preliminary hearing or an arraignment. (Depending upon your jurisdiction, you may be required to file a written entry of appearance with the court in addition to appearing in court with the defendant.) The defendant is usually notified of the time a place of the proceeding in the charging document, in the summons to appear, or during the Advisement.

10. PRETRIAL PROCESS

Every action taken between the time you enter your appearance and the trial is known as the pretrial process. However, there is a distinction, of sorts, between this process before and after the preliminary hearing. The process prior to the preliminary hearing may include filing motions to set a bond or modify a bond, obtaining and compelling discovery from the prosecution, conducting your own investigation, and filing various pretrial motions including, but not limited to, objecting to jurisdiction, asking for change of venue, and asking the court to recuse itself.

11. PRELIMINARY HEARING

In most jurisdictions, the next court proceeding in the felony process is the preliminary hearing. During this proceeding the prosecution presents its evidence to the court and the court determines if there is enough evidence to continue on to trial. The court makes a probable cause determination as to whether a felony has been committed and the defendant has committed the felony. While the defense is allowed to make argument regarding the evidence presented and cross-examine the prosecution's witnesses, the defense's ability to present evidence is often limited. Moreover, it is often not wise to present defense evidence at this stage, as presentation of such may reveal the defense strategy.

12. ARRAIGNMENT

The arraignment is a proceeding wherein the defendant is formally advised of the charges against him (they are read aloud to him by the court if he desires) and enters a plea on the record, in front of the judge. The choices of pleas to be entered are

- ▶ not guilty
- ▶ guilty as charged
- ▶ nolo contendere or no contest (which has the same effect of a guilty plea, but the plea cannot be used as evidence in a subsequent civil proceeding related to the same issue)
- ▶ guilty pursuant to a plea agreement with the prosecution
- ▶ to stand silent (thereafter the court enters a not guilty plea on the defendant's behalf)

If a "not guilty" plea is entered, the defendant should ask for a jury trial on the record. Entering a not guilty plea does not foreclose the option to later dispose of the case pursuant to a plea agreement. It is merely a formality that ensures the protection of the defendant's constitutional right to a speedy and public trial.

The effect of formerly entering a plea at arraignment is to start the clock running on the client's right to a speedy trial (speedy trial is a constitutional right; each jurisdiction has codified this right and you can find the rule of law in the statutes or the code). A trial date is usually chosen at this time. Other dates such as pretrial motion dates may be scheduled.

13. PRETRIAL CONFERENCE

The pretrial conference is a calendar-management hearing. It always occurs after arraignment. Either the court will automatically set one or one of the parties will request one. Some courts like them because it gives them insight as to whether the parties are working nicely and fairly with one another and there is a possibility of settlement.

During the conference, the court and the parties get a sense of whether the case is really going to trial.

In some jurisdictions, the court sets all future court dates during this proceeding. This includes a certain trial date and a date or dates to hear remaining pretrial motions. In addition, the court may set deadlines for the completion of discovery and for filing pretrial motions, and may advise the attorneys of various rules and expectations the court has regarding trial.

These conferences can be a useful tool for the defense as a reality check for the client, to rethink a reasonable offer. Once the client sees the court setting an actual trial date and imposing certain deadlines and restrictions on the parties, he may realize that the case is not going away and may reconsider his decision to plead not guilty.

14. TRIAL PREPARATION

Everything that occurs in the defense attorney's office after arraignment is known as trial preparation. It involves additional factual investigation, legal research, drafting and filing various pretrial motions, and preparing arguments, presentations, and evidence for trial.

15. PRETRIAL HEARINGS

Pretrial hearings are usually held closer to trial and are conducted in order to resolve all issues remaining before trial. The motions addressed at this point usually include motions to suppress evidence, motions in limine, and motions for sanctions for discovery violations.

These hearings act as the last reality check for the defendant who has a significant chance of being convicted at trial. It is usually during these hearings that he realizes he is about to cross the point of no return. Often, such a reality check may be necessary to convince an unrealistic client that he should accept a plea offer or begin plea negotiations.

16. TRIAL

The next proceeding is a trial. Trials can be to juries or to the court. The jury trial process includes, in order:

- ▶ Voir dire (choosing the jurors)
- ▶ Prosecution's opening statement
- ▶ Defendant's opening statement (if counsel chooses not to waive or reserve until the beginning of the defense case in chief)
- ▶ Prosecution's case-in-chief (which contains direct and cross-examination of each witness)
- ▶ Defendant's motion for judgment of acquittal
- ▶ Defendant's case-in-chief
- ▶ Jury instruction hearing
- ▶ Instructions to the jury by the court
- ▶ Prosecution's closing argument
- ▶ Defendant's closing argument
- ▶ Prosecution's rebuttal closing argument (if allowed)
- ▶ Jury deliberation
- ▶ Jury verdict

17. SENTENCING

Should the defendant be convicted, the next phase is sentencing. If he faces an aggravated sentence of incarceration, certain facts that form the basis for such may require an additional trial to the jury or to the court.

Some courts sentence the defendant immediately after the verdict and some postpone sentencing until a later date so that both sides can prepare arguments and evidence in favor of or against a particular sentence. Some sentences exceed the limits authorized by law; when this occurs, the excessive nature of the sentence will form the basis for challenging it.

18. APPEAL

If convicted after an evidentiary trial, the defendant may have the right to appeal certain court rulings. These include rulings on all pretrial matters, rulings on trial matters, and the sentence imposed.

If the defendant enters a guilty plea pursuant to a plea agreement, he may not have any right to appeal. However, the defendant always retains the right to appeal an egregious or illegal sentence. However, appeals are not addressed in this book.

CHAPTER 2

Initial Client Meeting and Interview

The initial client meeting occurs at approximately the eighth stage in the criminal justice process. The defendant or someone on his behalf has contacted you and either hired you (which means you have received a sum of money to retain your services), expressed an intent to hire you, or requested a meeting with you to discuss the matter and determine whether to engage your services.

Most attorneys meet with the defendant first in order to determine whether or not to take the case. With no money exchanged, the question becomes how much to discuss and review with the defendant and, ultimately, how much advice to give. Problems sometimes arise if the attorney decides not to take the case after such a meeting.

First, the potential client may rely on representations or advice you give, thereby creating a legal, contractual relationship, requiring the attorney to take some action on behalf of the client. For example, if you meet with a defendant in jail and promise to file a motion to modify his bond, you have an obligation to file the motion. Additionally, filing the motion under your signature ordinarily acts as an entry of appearance designating you as attorney of record for the defendant. Therefore, always consider how you are perceived by the defendant. Second, the attorney finds herself giving advice without getting payment for the services. I am confident you did not purchase this book to assist you in giving free criminal legal advice.

If you have a meeting with the client to determine whether you want to take the case, advise the client up front that you are not yet his attorney. Advise that you are not there to give legal advice. Explain that if you are not retained, you are not responsible if he acts upon any statements made by you during this meeting.

Inevitably, every potential client will want free advice. There is no bright line distinguishing how much to review or how much counseling to give. For the most part, it comes down to the attorney's comfort level with the client and the level of crime he is charged with.

If I perceive during the initial meeting that the client will be difficult, I likely will not take the case. Clients that are very demanding, accusing, and argumentative are often not worth my time. They inevitably require much more time and input than they are ever willing to pay for. You will know these people when you meet them.

You should never take a case that is above your experience level, unless you intend to enlist the help of a more experienced attorney. For example, you should not take a rape, homicide, tax evasion, or securities fraud case during your first year of practice. An attorney has an ethical obligation to effectively, competently, and zealously represent his client. It is very unlikely that you will have gained enough experience in your first year of criminal defense practice to competently handle the issues that arise in such high-stakes (I refer to them as such because the potential penalties are so great) or complex cases.

I have written most of this chapter assuming you have already been retained. I do not discuss how to find clients and how to decide whether to accept a client's retention.

WHAT SHOULD YOU DO PRIOR TO MEETING WITH THE CLIENT?

Prepare as best you can for the initial client meeting. Include the following in your preparations.

Determine Defendant's Charges

It is important to try to determine the charges. Never rely entirely on the defendant or the person who contacted you on the defendant's behalf (this could be family or friend) to accurately advise you of the pending charges. Previous clients have informed me that the pending charges were simple domestic violence matters when the charges actually involved matters such as attempted first-degree murder, kidnapping, or rape. That fact that the client has lived with, has slept with, or is related to the victim does not make the charge a "simple domestic matter."

TIPS FOR DETERMINING THE CLIENT'S CHARGES

1. *Ask the client or the person who initially makes contact.* Ask the nature of the charges during your initial contact with the defendant or the individ-

ual contacting you on his behalf regarding your representation. At the very least, try to determine the jurisdiction in which the charges are filed during this initial contact. Your questions might go like this:

▼ Do you know what you are charged with?

▼ Do you know if it is a felony or a misdemeanor?

▼ Do you know the court in which these charges are filed? If not, do you know who is prosecuting the case—the city, the county, the State of Colorado, the United States government?

▼ What does the piece of paper look like that notifies you of the charge and your court date? Does it say somewhere at the top of that piece of paper, "In the City of . . ., In the County of . . ., In the State of . . ."?

▼ Okay, because it says "In the City of Lakewood," I will assume the case is charged in municipal court. Since municipal courts in Colorado handle only traffic and misdemeanor matters, your charge is probably a misdemeanor.

▼ Does this piece of paper you have include a case number or filing number written upon it somewhere? Give me both of those numbers, please.

This exchange will likely provide you enough information to seek out the exact charge and its jurisdiction.

2. *Complaint and Information.* At some point early in any criminal proceeding, the client must be given a copy of the charging documents, often combined into one document called the Complaint and Information. This document notifies the defendant of the charge and criminal statute or code under which the crime is charged. This document is prepared by the investigating officer and issued to the defendant and to the court in cases of traffic tickets, some petit offenses, and some misdemeanor offenses. Otherwise, it is prepared by the prosecution and issued to the court, which is supposed to issue it to the defendant. Sometimes, the defendant does not receive the document, fails to provide the attorney with a copy, or, in most cases, misplaces it. If the defendant cannot provide you with a copy of his charging documents, you will need to obtain a copy. The Complaint and Information can be obtained in any of several places:

▼ *Criminal court clerk.* Ordinarily, these documents are public records and can be obtained from the criminal clerk of the jurisdiction in which the charges are filed (sometimes for a small fee). The court in which the charges are filed will always have a clerk's office, which has a physical address and public access in addition to a public access phone line. Some courts will have separate clerks for civil, criminal, appeals, probate, etc. Ask to speak with the court clerk who handles criminal matters. Give the clerk the defendant's name, and if you have it, case number. (Case information should be attainable through either.) At the very least, ask the clerk if you can have a printout of the computer screen describing the charge.

▼ *Prosecuting attorney.* If the clerk does not help, contact the prosecuting attorney's office and ask to photocopy or review their copy of the charging document. To find the prosecutor assigned to the case, call the prosecution attorney's office for the jurisdiction in which the charges were filed.

▼ Tell the person who answers the phone that you are an attorney trying to determine the prosecutor assigned to a case. The person on the other end of the line either will be able to help you or will refer you to someone in the office who can. Give that person the defendant's name, and if you have it, case number. (Case information should be attainable through either.)

▼ If the case has not yet been assigned to a prosecutor, ask to speak with someone who can give you a copy of the charging documents, or at a minimum advise you of the charges. Thanks to technology, any prosecutor (or his legal assistant) should be able to bring the matter up on a computer monitor and read to you the charge and its accompanying statute number. If, for whatever reason, the prosecutor will not give out copies of charging documents, ask him to tell you the exact charge and the statute under which the crime is charged.

I have never had either request refused. However, if both requests were denied by the prosecutor, I would file a motion with the jurisdiction advising the court of my difficulties in obtaining this easily accessible information from the prosecutor and asking for the court's prompt intervention Defendants have a constitutional right to know the exact nature of the crime with which they are being charged. Likewise, that right extends to any potential defense attorney. (After all, the prosecutor does not get to charge crimes and pursue prosecution in a vacuum.) Once the court hears of this flagrant abuse of the defendant's rights, you will no doubt get a court order directing the prosecution to provide you with this information.

▼ *Jail personnel.* If the defendant is in custody, contact the jail that houses inmates for the relevant jurisdiction and ask the jail personnel about the charges for which the defendant is being held. They usually have this information at their fingertips.

Determine the Elements That Form the Basis for the Charge

▶ *Review and copy the statutes or codes listed with the charge.* If you are able to determine the charges, review the statutes describing the violation. Copy the statutes at issue for your file.

▶ *Review and copy the uniform jury instruction or jury charge for the particular statutes.* Most state and federal jurisdictions have a set of uniform, or "pattern," jury instructions or jury charges describing the elements needed to establish the offense to the jury at trial. Jury instructions describe the applicable law in "plain English" or give direction to the persons serving on a jury concerning the law of a case. These uniform instructions are usually well-founded in case law and often have been written and prepared by a judicial body at the request and under the supervision of the jurisdiction's appellate courts or local bar association.

The instructions must be given to the jury at the close of all evidence. Failing to give these instructions to the jury or deviating from the exact wording of the instructions in giving them to the jury often invites prejudicial error by the court. If the court's prejudicial error acts to substantially deny a defendant of a constitutional right, then she is entitled to a retrial (if found guilty). (This information is discussed in more detail in Chapters 9 and 10.)

All practitioners should have their own hard copy of these uniform instructions. You may find uniform jury instructions on the Internet or through the various private computer research assistance services.

A sample Jury Instructions is included as Exhibit C on the enclosed CD-ROM. ➥

▶ *Take note of key language.* In reviewing the relevant instructions, pay particular attention to key language in the instructions such as "with the intent to," "knowing that," or "with reckless disregard to." These phrases often make the difference when it comes to the client's defense. I often tell my clients that these words are legal words that may act as an impediment to raising certain defenses, depending on the type of crime.

▼ *Strict liability crimes* have no defense other than that the crime never occurred or someone else did it. The prosecution need not prove that the act committed by the defendant was done with intent or knowingly. For example, statutory rape is a strict liability crime and has no defense other than that no crime was committed or that the defendant didn't do it. If the prosecution can establish that the defendant had sexual contact with a minor, then there is no defense such as consensual sexual contact (otherwise known as lack of intent) or lack of knowledge regarding the victim's age (otherwise known as knowingly committed the crime). In other words, proof of statutory rape does not require that defendant *intended* to have sexual contact with a minor or *knowingly* had sexual contact with a minor. Therefore, it may not be a defense that the defendant did not know the age of the victim. The mere proof of the occurrence of the act makes the defendant guilty.

▼ Some jurisdictions limit the types of defenses that can be run for *general intent crimes*. A general intent crime requires proof that the defendant intended to commit the conduct charged but requires no additional element of intent such as premeditation or knowledge, whereas specific intent requires that the defendant intended to commit the conduct charged and an additional element of intent. For instance, some jurisdictions do not allow the defense of voluntary intoxication (knowingly consuming an intoxicating substance thereby becoming so intoxicated that the defendant could not knowingly appreciate the nature of his actions) if the crime requires only proof of general intent.

▼ In most jurisdictions, premeditated first-degree murder is a crime of *specific intent* because the defendant must have both intended and premeditated the murder. In a jurisdiction that makes the distinction between specific and general intent, a defense of voluntary intoxication will be allowed in the prosecution of premeditated murder and it will not be allowed in the prosecution of an unplanned murder.

Determine the Potential Penalty the Charge Carries

Next, review the criminal code for the potential penalties that the defendant will face should there be a judgment of guilty as charged. Determine if the crimes charged subject the defendant to mandatory imprisonment or if the charges carry a non-prison/jail sanction (probation, diversion, deferred judgment, suspended imposition of sentence, etc.).

WHAT SHOULD YOU COVER DURING THE FIRST CLIENT MEETING?

The following areas of inquiry may be relevant during the initial meeting. These topics are in no particular order.

Show Empathy

Try to show some empathy no matter what horrendous thing the defendant is accused of committing. You have to earn a level of trust in order to effectively represent your client. You need to know everything about the client. If the client does not trust you, he may not be entirely forthcoming with you. Without trust, you can not adequately and effectively represent the client.

Starting off with compassion for the client is a good way to start building this relationship of trust. You might say something like this:

> I am sorry this is happening to you. I am sorry you are facing circumstances that require you to seek my help. I do not yet know your background or the entire circumstances that brought you to me, but I want you to know I will do whatever I can to ensure that your rights are protected and that the system treats you as fairly as it can.

Explain the Attorney–Client Privilege

Explain that everything the client tells you during your meetings is privileged and confidential, that no one is allowed to know what you and the client discuss. This means that no one can force either of you to reveal the content of your discussions. And this privilege extends to everyone associated with the defense team.

Warn the client that the privilege can be lost if she reveals matters discussed in your meetings to other people—and this usually includes spouses.

Explain the Importance of Secrecy

Tell the client the following:

▶ Do not discuss your charges or the facts of your case with anyone. This includes your family and friends.

▶ If asked about your case, refuse to answer questions. In doing so, be polite and explain that your attorney has advised you not to discuss the matter with anyone.

▶ You cannot discuss the case, because anyone you discuss it with can be brought into court and forced to testify about your conversations.

I often tell the story of a client of mine who was charged with rape. We claimed that he had consensual sex with the alleged victim. Unfortunately, when asked by his friends outside of my presence, he denied ever having sex with the woman. The prosecutor later brought the friends in to trial to testify against the defendant after he testified that he had in fact had consensual sex with the alleged victim. The prosecutor consequently argued to the jury that defendant's complete denial to his friends was evidence of his guilty mind.

Advise against Speaking to the Judge or Prosecutor

I also advise the client to refrain from contacting the judge or prosecutor prior to any plea or conviction. I have been surprised at the number of defendants who write the prosecutor or judge from jail asking for leniency. Clients often make incriminating statements in these letters that can later be used against them at trial or at the time of sentencing.

This advice is equally applicable to the client's friends and family. Letters and statements providing support or requesting leniency are appropriate, but only after the defendant is convicted of something. Until that point, everything said to the court and prosecutor should be screened through the defendant's attorney.

Stress the Importance of Honesty

Tell the client to tell the truth at all costs.

I advise my client that I cannot effectively represent her unless she is completely honest with me about everything, including her personal background. I remind her that everything that is discussed stays between us and is protected by the attorney–client privilege. I tell the client that if she tells me that she is going to lie, then I cannot present her lie to the jury. I add that if she lies to me and I find out through the course of investigation that she is lying, then I can no longer pursue the defense supported by the lie. It is illegal for me to suborn perjury, and I cannot and will not support her if she intends to lie on the stand.

If she lies, I will attempt to withdraw from her case. If the court refuses my request, the law requires me to put her on the stand and let her testify in the narrative. In other words, I cannot directly ask her questions that elicit her lies. I merely will say, after advising the court I intend to have my client testify in the narrative, "Is there something you would like to say to the jury?" (There have been attempts in various jurisdictions to revise this narrative testimony rule over the years. Make certain to review the local ethical rules in regard to proceeding without suborning perjury from your client.)

Review the Defendant's Criminal History

Have the defendant give a detailed review of his criminal history, including any juvenile convictions and every arrest. If the defendant indicates that he has never been convicted of a crime, do not accept that as the final answer. Some defendants believe that juvenile offenses, DUIs or DWIs, driving while under suspended or restricted license, and various misdemeanor offenses are not considered criminal convictions—but they are under the law and in the eyes of the court.

Previous convictions become relevant in determining the penalty that the court may impose if a conviction result. (This includes previous traffic, petty, misdemeanor, and felony offenses.) Sometimes previous convictions require the court to impose a mandatory sentence.

━━o

━━━━━━━━━━━━━━━━━━━━━━━━━━━━━━━━━━━

TIPS FOR FOR DETERMINING CRIMINAL HISTORY

Question the defendant as follows to determine criminal history:

1. "Have you ever been arrested?"
   - ▼ "What happened with the case after your arrest?"
   - ▼ "Was the case dismissed without prosecution?"
   - ▼ "Was the case dismissed after you completed a deferred judgment or sentence, a suspended sentence, or some sort of program required of you by the court or prosecutor?"
2. "Have you ever had contact with law enforcement for any reason?"
3. "Have you ever been brought to court for any reason?"
4. "I understand that you were advised that your juvenile record was sealed. However, if I am going to properly advise you of the potential penalties that you face, I must know all about your juvenile record. I promise, anything you tell me about any juvenile crimes or arrests will not go outside of this room without your permission."
5. "Have you ever gone to jail? How long were you in custody?"
6. "Have you ever served time in prison?"
7. "Have you ever served time in a juvenile detention center? How long were you in custody?"

RELEVANCE OF CRIMINAL HISTORY: BAIL BOND

Criminal history is important in obtaining a bond (also referred to in some jurisdictions as "bail") or reducing one already imposed. I cannot count the number of times I have requested my client's bond be reduced only to be rebutted by a prosecutor's complaint: "But Your Honor, the defendant's NCIC report reveals he has been arrested 12 times in his life and convicted twice for aggravated battery and convicted once for . . ." NCIC is the National Criminal Information Computer. It's a rap sheet maintained by the feds that includes every contact with the legal system.

If the defendant truly has no record or has a minor record (at most, traffic offenses and one misdemeanor offense), his chances of being granted a reasonable bail increase.

A sample NCIC Rap Sheet is included as Exhibit D on the enclosed CD-ROM. A sample Rap Sheet Prepared by Court Administration is included as Exhibit E on the enclosed CD-ROM. ━o

RELEVANCE OF CRIMINAL HISTORY: EVIDENCE

Criminal history is also important because it may appear as evidence against the defendant in his trial. In some jurisdictions, if defendant takes the witness stand, every crime for which he has ever been convicted may be introduced as impeachment evidence against him. In other jurisdictions, the prosecutor may introduce only those crimes that are relevant to the defendant's truth and veracity should he take the stand, i.e., crimes of honesty or felonies. In still other jurisdictions, the prosecution may introduce such evidence only if defendant raises the subject (for example, defendant places into evidence his good character or testifies he has never been in trouble with the law).

Even if the defendant chooses not to testify, evidence of the same or similar conduct may be introduced as evidence in the prosecution's case in chief in order to establish proof of motive, opportunity, intent, plan, knowledge, identity, or absence of mistake or accident.

RELEVANCE OF CRIMINAL HISTORY: SENTENCE

Criminal history is relevant to any current criminal case because potential penalties are often based upon past convictions. Recent trends in sentencing law make previous convictions relevant to the jury's verdict should the defendant be charged with a crime such as possession of a firearm after a previous felony conviction. In that instance, the jury will be asked to find beyond a reasonable doubt that defendant has a previous felony conviction.

Many jurisdictions sentence defendants based upon their criminal records, with the potential sentencing range increasing in cases where the defendant has prior convictions (most often prior felonies are used to enhance the sentence, but some jurisdictions use prior misdemeanors to enhance as well).

Some jurisdictions even allow the sentencing judge to impose "aggravated sentences" or "upward departure sentences" when the defendant has previous convictions for the same or similar offense. For example, a defendant charged with a sex crime or a sexually motivated crime who has a prior statutorily defined sex offense conviction may be subject to a mandatory aggravated sentence. Harsher penalties for second-time DUI/DWI convictions is another example of this type of enhanced punishment scheme.

Review the Charging Document

If no charging document is available, review with the defendant the charges that you have discovered during your preinterview preparation, as discussed earlier in this chapter.

If a copy of the charging document is available, ask the defendant if he knows what he is charged with. This provides an opportunity to judge the defendant's level of sophistication and his level of competency (both mental and as to the criminal justice system).

Sometimes the defendant's knowledge of his charges is all that you will have available at this first meeting.

Review the Elements of the Crime

The charging documents often do not adequately or simply describe the elements of the crime charged. Their purpose is merely to put a defendant on notice of the crime charged. Some jurisdictions refer to this as "notice pleading."

The charge is often stated in the Complaint and Information as follows:

Scott W. Storey, District Attorney for the first judicial district of the State of Colorado, in the name and by the authority of the People of the State of Colorado, informs the court of the following offenses committed, or triable, in the county of Jefferson:

Count 1—Possession of a Controlled Substance—Schedule II: 1 Gram or Less (F6)

On July 14, 2005, Defendant, John Doe, unlawfully and knowingly possessed one gram or less of a material, compound, mixture, or preparation that contained methamphetamine, a schedule II controlled substance; in violation of section 18-18-405(1),(2.3)(a)(I), C.R.S.

In reviewing this charge with the defendant, I say, "They claim you were in possession or control of less than a gram of methamphetamine on July 14, 2004." I then review all of the elements and relevant definitions that are set out in the pattern jury instructions of Colorado (if they are available) and answer any questions the defendant may have regarding the same.

For the above charge, the Colorado elements of proof as they appear in the pattern jury instruction for this crime (and as I would review them with the client) are as follows:

1. That the defendant,
2. In the State of Colorado, on July 14, 2004, in the County of Jefferson,
3. Knowingly or intentionally,
4. Possessed one gram or less,
5. Of the schedule II controlled substance, methamphetamine.

A person acts "knowingly" with respect to conduct or to a circumstance described by a statute defining an offense when he is aware that his conduct is of such nature or that such circumstance exists. A person acts "knowingly" with respect to a result of his conduct when he is aware that his conduct is practically certain to cause the result.

A person acts "with intent" when his conscious objective is to cause the specific result proscribed by the statue defining the offense. It is immaterial whether or not the result actually occurred.

"Controlled substance" means a drug or other substance or an immediate precursor which is declared to be a controlled substance under Sections 18-18-203 through 18-18-207 C.R.S., including methamphetamine.

"Possession" as used in these instructions does not necessarily mean ownership, but does mean the actual, physical possession, or the immediate and knowing dominion or control over the object or the thing allegedly possessed. "Possession" need not be exclusive, provided that each possessor, should there be more than one, actually knew of the presence of the object, or thing possessed, and exercised actual physical control or immediate, knowing dominion or control over it.

Address the Defendant's Questions

LEGALITY OF THE CHARGES

You will inevitably be asked by the defendant why certain acts with which he is charged are criminal. As an example, I was once asked by a client why possession of images of underage boys engaged in certain lewd acts was criminal when the same images could be found in books at the local library. Though I have never perused the shelves of the local library for these images, I was hesitant to discount the defendant's claim. I responded, "I don't know why the legislature criminalizes certain acts. I am just here to represent you on this charge. Perhaps you should contact your local legislator and discuss that with her."

As an additional example, when my clients are charged with high-level drug offenses for possession of small quantities of drugs or with an attempted drug-manufacturing crime for purchasing boxes of cold medicine (for which the constitutional issues have been well settled), my response to such questions includes, "I hear you, man, you're preaching to the choir. I don't like the charge, maybe even the judge won't like it, but the legality of the statute making this a crime is well settled. Should you get convicted, you should take the matter up with the appeals court. For now, let's work on making this charge go away or getting a less severe penalty."

Sometimes a constitutional issue will arise with the particular conduct charged. In the rare event that happens, advise the client about addressing the issue on the motion to dismiss. (Motions to dismiss based upon constitutional grounds are addressed in Chapter 5.)

Sometimes, nothing you can say will ease the client's mind. In that event, just let the client vent. Sometimes the best thing we can do for our clients is to just listen to them. Often, that is all they really want from us.

POTENTIAL PENALTIES

The client will likely ask what potential penalties she faces. (You will have determined the potential penalties prior to the client meeting.) Preface your explanation by saying, "I am not saying that you will receive this sentence. I am merely advising you of the worst-case scenario." Let the client know that the potential penalty may increase if she has criminal convictions that she has forgotten to discuss.

Depending upon the severity of the crime, type of criminal conviction, and the jurisdiction, typical penalties may include one or a combination of the following:

► *Fine.* The court may order the defendant to pay a certain sum of money by a certain time.

► *Restitution.* The defendant may be ordered to pay a sum of money to the victim as compensation for the victim's loss. Most jurisdictions now require mandatory restitution to include certain costs incurred by various law enforcement entities, such as laboratory testing or extradition expenses (I once had a client ordered to repay Sedgwick County, Kansas, over $3,500 for extraditing him via a private plane from Las Vegas).

► *Community service.* This type of punishment requires the defendant to work a number of hours for a local charity, nonprofit organization, or court-approved entity without compensation. The defendant repays the community for his crime by performing some useful public service.

► *Probation.* Instead of spending time in jail or in prison, the defendant is placed on probation for a period of time. She must not get into any trouble with the law and must follow any conditions the court imposes. The defendant may also be required to

▼ Report to the jurisdiction's probation department on a regular basis.

▼ Refrain from using alcohol or any drug unless prescribed by a physician.

▼ Undergo random drug screens at the defendant's expense.

▼ Attend anger-management classes.

▼ Attend driver-safety classes.

▼ Attend counseling.

▼ Successfully complete a substance-abuse-treatment program.

▼ Attend Narcotics Anonymous or Alcoholics Anonymous meetings for a designated period of time and a designated number of times per week or month.

▼ Obtain a high school diploma or its equivalent (GED).

▼ Live in a halfway house (described below) for a specified period of time.

▼ Pay restitution ordered by the court.

▼ Write an apology letter to the victim.

▼ Pay probation supervision fees (to help the jurisdiction recoup the cost of the supervision expenses).

For many of these, the idea is that there are programs in the community that support offender reformation without incarceration.

▶ *Incarceration.* Incarceration comes in various forms:

▼ *Jail.* Traffic offenses, petty convictions, misdemeanor convictions, and low-severity-level felonies are punished by incarceration in jail. Jails are run by the local municipalities (cities and counties). The amount of time served in this facility is at the discretion of the court. Ordinarily, however, the court's discretion is confined to a certain window of time for each crime pursuant to statute. For example, the maximum incarceration penalty a Colorado court can impose for a petty offense is six months in the county jail. The maximum incarceration penalty that can be imposed for a non-DUI traffic infraction is one year in the county jail. And the maximum incarceration penalty that can be imposed for a misdemeanor is 24 months in the county jail.

▼ *State or federal prison.* Prison is reserved for felony and federal crimes. The length of the sentence is prescribed by statute for each crime for which the defendant is convicted, though some jurisdictions give judges wide discretion as to the amount of time that can be imposed. As with misdemeanors, the statutes prescribe a sentencing range for the particular offense. For example, Colorado assigns each felony crime a severity level ranging from 1, the highest, to 6, the lowest. For a severity level 6 crime, the court has discretion to sentence the defendant from one to four years. For a severity level 5 crime, the sentencing discretion ranges from one to eight years.

If applicable, discuss the period of parole. Most jurisdictions require that a defendant be supervised for a period of time on parole after he has served his prison sentence.

▼ *Halfway house.* This is a government-run or -funded facility in which the defendant is sentenced to live for a period of time. It is different from incarceration as the defendant is allowed to interact with the community. Inmates are allowed to have jobs and participate in certain activities of free society. However, all activities have to be approved and monitored. The inmates are required to sleep in the facility. It is called "halfway" because it represents a place between full incarceration and living freely. It is a reintegration incarceration, wherein the defendant is required to show that he is amenable to less supervision or absolute freedom. Halfway houses are utilized by municipalities, states, and the federal system.

▼ *Boot camp.* These incarceration programs are designed to be like military boot camps. The defendant is sentenced to complete a period of time in the boot camp. Ordinarily, incarceration in these facilities is reserved for younger adult offenders and offenders who have been convicted of low-severity-level offenses or nonviolent offenses. The inmates march, exercise, and address their guards/trainers like they are military superiors. They attend classes on various subjects, including GED classes and drug treatment and education classes. Often, when an inmate graduates from the program, he is released back into the community and placed on probation. The idea is to teach the defendant discipline and self-respect. The belief follows that those traits will help reform the defendant and reduce recidivism.

Review Discovery with the Defendant

Criminal discovery includes all documents, police reports, audio and video-tape recordings, CDs, DVDs, diagrams, reports of physical and mental exams, reports of scientific exams and tests, witness lists, transcripts of grand jury or inquisition testimony, demonstrative evidence, and physical evidence in the custody or control of the prosecution or its agents (which includes law enforcement officers and anyone working for law enforcement)—essentially, any tangible thing that is relevant to include defendant in the involvement of the crime (inculpatory evidence), to exclude the defendant (exculpatory evidence), or to set punishment. Defendants have a right to see all discoverable information.

A sample Police Report is included as Exhibit F on the enclosed CD-ROM. ➥

AFFIDAVITS

If the case involves a felony, at this point you may have only the affidavit of probable cause or the affidavit in support of the arrest or search warrant. These are sworn statements, usually sworn to by the lead or supervising detective. They summarize the facts that the state relies upon in bringing the charges and establish the initial probable cause for the court in order to justify detaining the defendant on the charges.

These documents can be obtained from the criminal court clerk, the judge, or the prosecutor's office. They are ordinarily in the public record (although the court can order them sealed from public view in high-profile matters) and can be obtained without having to formally enter as the attorney of record on the case.

A sample Affidavit of Probable Cause (also known as an Affidavit in Support of Warrantless Arrest) is included as Exhibit G on the enclosed CD-ROM. ➥

CRIMINAL DISCOVERY AS IT DIFFERS FROM CIVIL DISCOVERY

Criminal discovery differs from civil discovery, in part because the defendant's freedom is in jeopardy and because the plaintiff is a governmental entity. Criminal proceedings invoke far more constitutional rights than civil proceedings do.

As such, the defendant is not required to go searching for the evidentiary issues. He is entitled to everything relevant to include him in the involvement of the crime, to exclude him in the involvement of the crime, or to set his punishment. The defense does not have to conduct depositions or submit interrogatories, requests for production of documents, or requests for admissions to have access to the prosecution's discovery. The prosecutor has a legal duty to disclose all inculpatory and exculpatory evidence.[1]

Most jurisdictions do not allow depositions or allow them only upon a finding by the court that the testimony of the deposed witness is material and it is necessary to take the deposition in order to prevent a failure of justice, e.g., the witness is dying, is on the verge of becoming incompetent, or is highly likely to leave the jurisdiction before trial.

Although many jurisdictions have reciprocal criminal discovery rules (which means defendant has an obligation to disclose certain information to the prosecution), the defendant's duty to reciprocate discovery is often limited to allowing the prosecution to inspect exams, experiments, diagrams, and physical evidence that is material and that the defense intends to produce at trial.

GIVING DEFENDANT COPIES OF DISCOVERY

You might give the defendant copies of discovery documents to review along with you and to keep for himself. Sometimes defendants can find hidden gems in the discovery that you have overlooked.

If the defendant is in custody, use your judgment regarding whether to give a copy of these documents to the defendant. Other inmates, and sometimes jail guards for that matter, may read through or even steal a fellow inmate's discovery. This often happens in high-profile cases or cases in which the defendant is charged with rape, kidnapping, or aggravated robbery (charges that carry a significant sentence). Copies of the discovery in the wrong hands may subject the defendant to hatred, ridicule, and even violence.

Stolen discovery can also be used by fellow inmates to lend credibility to jailhouse confessions alleged by these inmates to have been given by your client. These inmates create these fake confessions to get more lenient treatment for themselves. They approach the police or the prosecutor and contend that the defendant made incriminating statements to them about his case. They may claim facts that appear in the discovery as factual statements made to them by the defendant.

Another concern is that the press may publish information obtained from stolen or leaked discovery. No matter your client's guilt or innocence, you do not want specific facts of your case to be published in the press. It may contaminate the jury pool.

---

[1] *See Brady v. Maryland*, 373 U.S. 83 (1963); *United States v. Agurs*, 427 U.S. 97 (1976).

OBTAINING ADDITIONAL DISCOVERY

Discuss with the defendant the methods of obtaining additional discovery according to your jurisdiction's practices and procedures. If the defendant has been in jail for a few days, assume she has been conversing with the "jailhouse lawyers" (inmates who give legal advice, usually bad, to other inmates). They may have told your client that her lawyer should file a motion for discovery. Sometimes these motions are necessary and sometimes not.

The prosecutor owes you discovery documents even without an order so long as you have formerly entered your appearance as attorney of record in the case.[2] I have found that a simple letter to the prosecutor requesting copies of all discoverable information works quite well. Only when informal requests go unanswered do I file a motion to compel discovery and attach my letter to the motion as an exhibit to show the court the prosecutor is being naughty.

In Jefferson County, Colorado, one of the jurisdictions in which I practice, attorneys need merely make a phone call to the district attorney's discovery department. A fax of an entry of appearance or a court order of appearance will suffice as an official discovery request. My practice aside, make certain you are aware of the local rules regarding discovery. (You can find these in your jurisdiction's statutes or code.)

Ask for the Client's Side of the Story

I do not always want a detailed recitation of the client's story at the beginning of our first meeting. This is because I may be stuck with the initial story he tells me. If he tells me that he committed the crime, I cannot later assist him to testify if he did not. That would be suborning perjury. (On many occasions, the client tells me one thing at the first meeting and then the complete opposite at trial.) Instead, I have the client review the discovery and the preliminary hearing testimony before I ask for his side of the story. It gives him some time to see the information everyone has, which encourages him to tell the truth. It also gives me some time to review the discovery and to grasp the evidence presented by the prosecution at the preliminary hearing in order to help massage the defendant's story out of him. (I do not have to believe the client's story. I just have to sell it to the trier of fact.)

During the initial meetings, you may ask certain questions of the client, searching for answers to various "bad facts" (facts that are ugly or contrary to the defense strategy) that appear in the discovery. (You can do this even if you are trying to avoid a detailed narrative.) For example:

▶ "If you weren't drinking, can you explain the empty beer cans the police say they found all over the kitchen counter?"

---

[2] *Id.*

► "If you did not hit him, how did he get the gash across his forehead?"

► "Why would she say you raped her when you are saying the sex was consensual?"

Explain Upcoming Proceedings

Advise the defendant of the proceedings yet to come and how these hearings usually work. The key criminal proceedings are often in the following order:

► *Advisement* (often happens within the first 48 hours of arrest wherein the defendant is advised by the court of the charges against him and of certain constitutional rights)

► *First Appearance and Appearance of Counsel*

► *Preliminary hearing* (if felony charges)

► *Arraignment*

► *Pretrial conference*

► *Pretrial hearings* (motions hearings)

► *Trial*

ADVISEMENT AND FIRST APPEARANCE

The Advisement is often the first proceeding after the defendant's arrest or receipt of summons. It usually occurs within 24 hours of arrest. Failure to bring the accused before a judge within a reasonable time or the time proscribed by statute may result in the defendant's release without prosecution and without the need to post bail. (However, the prosecutor has until the expiration of the statute of limitations to file charges.)

In the Advisement, the defendant appears before a judge and is advised of the charges against him, certain constitutional rights (usually his *Miranda* rights), and the amount of bail. After this, the court will set a date for the client to appear with counsel.

If the defendant is in custody, either the defendant is transported from the jail to this proceeding, the proceeding is held in the jail, or the defendant appears in court from the jail via closed circuit television.

If you do appear at this proceeding, your job is simple:

► Enter your appearance on the record (and in writing if required by the court)

► Listen to the charges as read by the court

► Enter your client's plea

► Ask for bail to be set or argue for a lower bail if the court is open to such requests at that time. The court has broad discretion in addressing bail and may take into account the following:

- ▼ The nature of the crime
- ▼ The weight of the evidence
- ▼ Family ties
- ▼ Employment
- ▼ Financial resources
- ▼ Character and mental condition
- ▼ Community ties
- ▼ Prior convictions
- ▼ Prior failures to appear in court
- ▼ Prior bond forfeitures

Sometimes the defendant will appear at the Advisement without counsel. The court will then set a First Appearance or an Appearance of Counsel in order to give the defendant an opportunity to appear with an attorney and set the matter for future proceedings.

You will often not meet with your clients until after the Advisement. (Advisement and First Appearance are discussed more fully in Chapter 3.)

PRELIMINARY HEARING

If charged with a felony, the next pivotal stage is the preliminary hearing. The preliminary hearing is a proceeding in which the prosecution presents its evidence to the court and the court determines if there is sufficient evidence to hold a trial. In explaining the proceeding to the defendant, emphasize that the proceeding is not a trial. Too often, clients mistakenly believe that the case will be thrown out at preliminary hearing. In reality, maybe one case in 500 is dismissed by the court at the preliminary hearing.

PROSECUTION'S ROLE The prosecution always has the burden of proof in criminal cases. The burden of proof required of the prosecution at this hearing is very low. It is not proof beyond a reasonable doubt. The prosecutor's burden of proof requires him to prove to the court that there is probable cause to believe the crime has been committed and probable cause to believe the defendant committed the crime.

Sometimes, I describe the prosecutor's burden of proof to the defendant this way: "The judge need only determine that if we went to trial right now on the evidence that was presented, there is a 51 percent chance that a jury would find you guilty after listening to this evidence."

The court must view all evidence in the light most favorable to the prosecution. The court does not judge the strength of the prosecution's case or whether the prosecutor can prove the defendant guilty beyond a reasonable doubt at trial. Most jurisdictions relax the rules of evidence for preliminary hearings. Often, the prosecution is allowed to present its whole case based upon hearsay evidence.

DEFENSE COUNSEL'S ROLE The defense is allowed to cross-examine the prosecution's witnesses, make argument with regard to the prosecution meeting its burden of proof, and present a limited amount of evidence. Cross-examination should be used to box the witnesses in to certain points (from which they can not deviate from at the time of trial or else you will impeach them with a transcript of their preliminary hearing testimony) and to explore issues not necessarily clear or apparent in the discovery. Should their testimony differ later, their preliminary hearing cross-examination testimony can be used to impeach them.

I advise the client during the initial meeting that I probably will not be presenting witnesses at the preliminary hearing. Doing so would be an unnecessary revelation of our trial strategy. I emphasize, however, that I will be attacking the prosecution's case by cross-examining its witnesses and making argument to the court about the prosecution having not met its burden of proof of probable cause. I was taught that presentation of defense evidence through calling witnesses at this stage unnecessarily reveals the defense theory of the case to the prosecution; that witnesses should only be called if there is no other way to explore what the witness will say at trial. (In the thousands of cases I have defended, I have always found another way to explore what the witness will say at trial.)

Most courts will not permit the defense to call witnesses to testify to matters outside the scope of matters testified to by the prosecution's witnesses or which may duplicate the evidence presented by the prosecution's witnesses. In other words, the court restricts your ability to go on a discovery fishing expedition. (You can always have your investigator interview the witness outside of court.)

Under no circumstances should the defendant testify at the preliminary hearing. Doing so will cause the defendant to waive his Fifth Amendment right against self-incrimination.

ARRAIGNMENT

The arraignment is a proceeding in which the defendant enters a formal plea on the record. The choices of pleas to be entered are

► Not guilty

► Guilty as charged

► Nolo contendere, or no contest (which has the same effect as a guilty plea, but nolo contendere cannot be used as evidence in a subsequent civil proceeding related to the same issue)

▶   Guilty pursuant to a written plea agreement with the prosecution

The defendant may also enter no plea and stand silent, in which case the court enters a not guilty plea on the defendant's behalf. A defendant will stand silent if there is an issue as to the court's jurisdiction, e.g., something wrong with the charging document.

The effect of formerly entering a plea at arraignment is to start the clock running on the client's right to a speedy trial. The Sixth Amendment of the Constitution provides that "in all criminal prosecutions the accused shall enjoy the right to a speedy trial." This protection is applicable to the states through the 14th Amendment.

Each jurisdiction has its own procedural statute that regulates the time in which a criminal defendant must be brought to trial. In Colorado, for instance, a defendant charged with a felony must be brought to trial within 180 days after entering a plea of not guilty. This right can be waived by the defendant. It is often waived to provide counsel more time to prepare for trial or to negotiate a plea agreement.

A trial date is usually set by the judge at the time of arraignment. If not, the court will set a pretrial conference at a later date to set the trial date and address and schedule any other outstanding matters to be resolved before trial.

What is important to tell the client about this stage is that it involves entering a formal plea of not guilty, if a plea agreement has not yet been reached, and requesting the matter be set for a jury trial. If I know that the client wants me to pursue a plea offer from the prosecution, I tell him, "I know you want a plea offer, but I have to plead you not guilty and request a jury trial in order to protect your constitutional right to a speedy and public jury trial should plea negotiations fail."

PRETRIAL CONFERENCE

Pretrial conferences, at which the parties discuss the anticipated length of the trial and the likelihood that the matter will ever go to trial, help the court and the parties set the calendar for the case. This is a housecleaning tool used by the court and counsel to keep the case on track and resolve any pretrial issues. Sometimes a court will set several pretrial conferences throughout the course of the case at either party's request. These conferences are usually held some time after the Arraignment (six to eight weeks) and before the trial (four to eight weeks). Pretrial conferences can be set by the court or set at the request of either party. If a trial date is not established at the time of arraignment (by motion of the parties), the court will set a trial date during this proceeding.

Some courts require a pretrial order that sets forth all resolved and unresolved issues to date. Each party is required to sign off on the order. I often request a pretrial conference to buy time to negotiate a better plea offer or to continue talking my client into taking the plea. If the request is granted, the court often requires the client to waive his right to a speedy trial so that the client cannot later claim that the delays violated his right to a speedy trial.

PRETRIAL HEARING

Next, I explain how and when pretrial motions—which include suppression of evidence motions, motions to dismiss, and motions to exclude certain evidence (motions in limine)—will be argued to the court. Any proceeding that occurs between the arraignment and the trial may be referred to as a pretrial hearing.

TRIAL

If the client asks, I give a rough explanation of the trial procedure and what to expect. But generally, I reserve in-depth trial procedure explanations for a time closer to trial because of the extensive amount of information to be covered with the client during the initial meeting.

Give a Case Timeline

Advise the client of a timeline on which you expect the case to flow. (It is always best to err on the side of longer time estimates to the client. The client will love you if you can get the case resolved sooner.)

▶   Most misdemeanor cases can take six months or more for a resolution.

▶   Felony cases can easily take up to a year before resolution.

A timeline is important because it impresses upon the defendant the seriousness of the matter and enables him to plan his life, if out of custody, or resolve himself to a potentially significant jail stay if in custody.

Most defendants are initially frustrated with the length of time it takes to resolve a case. It helps to explain to them that the timeline is designed to ensure that their rights to due process are protected. It takes time to compile the necessary evidence and develop a strategy to proceed to trial or effectively negotiate a plea.

Most prosecutors are not realistic or just not willing to entertain plea negotiations until the eve of trial or the court ordered plea cutoff. They can be lazy and sometimes do not learn much about their cases until the last minute. It is not until they really know their case that they realize that a plea offer should be extended.

Explain the Decisions the Client Must Make

Tell the client that, as his attorney, you make the decisions regarding what motions to file, the process by which discovery is obtained, the process by which case investigation is conducted, the procedural strategy, and the trial strategy. Then explain that the following decisions belong exclusively to the client:

▶ *Whether to have a preliminary hearing.*

▶ *Whether to approach the prosecution about a plea bargain.*

▶ *Whether to enter or accept a plea.*

▶ *Whether to have the trial before a jury or the judge (bench trial).*

▶ *Whether to run an entrapment defense.* An entrapment defense tells the trier of fact that the defendant committed the crime, but that she would not have done it had the police not illegally enticed her to do it. This defense is very risky because it requires the defendant to admit that she committed the crime charged.

▶ *Whether to run a "lesser-included offense" defense.* This defense alleges that the defendant is not guilty of the crime charged but is guilty of a similar, less severe crime. The defense asks the jury to convict the defendant, but on the less severe crime. Proof of the essential elements of the crime charged necessarily establishes the elements required to prove the lesser offense.[3] An example of an opening statement for such a defense:

> The crime of aggravated burglary requires that the prosecution prove that the defendant entered the home with the intent to commit a theft from the home. Defendant in fact entered the home, but he did not commit the crime of aggravated burglary. He committed the lesser-included crime of criminal trespass. He had no intent to commit a theft in the home. He merely entered the house to flee from the pursuing police. He thought the house was empty.

The charging document may charge defendant with a primary offense and a "lesser included" or "in the alternative" offense. In that instance, you ask the jury to find defendant guilty of the lesser of the two defenses.

▶ *Whether to run a defense that admits defendant's presence at the crime scene, but denies his guilt.* In this circumstance, defense counsel advises the jury that the defense does not deny that defendant was present at the scene, but explains that the defendant was merely an innocent bystander. An example of an opening statement for such a defense:

> Defendant was in fact at the Borden house at the time of the murders. But as he waited in the car while the murder was committed, he had no idea that his codefendants lacked permission to enter the home. The defendant had no idea they were about to commit the robbery or the murder that followed. He is not guilty of the crime of felony murder because he lacked the requisite intent to commit the robbery.

---

[3] *Armintrout v. People*, 864 P.2d 576 (Colo. 1993).

▶ *Whether to run an insanity or mental disease or defect defense.* It sounds oxymoronic, doesn't it—asking a crazy person whether to run the "crazy" defense? But most jurisdictions require a defendant's permission to use such defenses. It is like running a lesser-included defense. In an insanity defense, the defendant admits to committing the crime, but claims that she lacked the requisite mental capacity to be in control of her faculties.

▶ *Witness tampering.* Tell the defendant that he must not approach any witness about the case. To do so is a crime called witness tampering or witness intimidation.

In order to avoid an allegation of witness tampering, advise the defendant to not contact any of the witnesses listed by the State, even if the witness may be favorable to the defense. In some jurisdictions, the court will issue a restraining order forbidding the defendant from having contact with any of the witnesses listed in the charging document or endorsed by the prosecution. In case there is not a restraining order, and defendant is living with the alleged victim or other witnesses, defendant should move out.

Advise the defendant that if you feel it necessary to obtain additional statements or verify statements that appear in the discovery, you will be contacting the witnesses through your investigator, in order to avoid any allegation of witness tampering.

I tell my clients that I do not want them speaking to any potential defense witnesses about the case in order to avoid any appearance of impropriety or any argument by the state that the defendant has coerced, implanted, or enticed the witness's testimony.

These admonitions are equally applicable to the defendant's family and friends. Any attempt to contact the witnesses by the defendant's family and friends is seen by the prosecutor and the court as if the defendant made the contact himself, and may be interpreted as witness tampering.

WHAT INFORMATION SHOULD YOU OBTAIN DURING THE FIRST MEETING?

General Client Information

It is good to begin the interview with simple questions involving the following information:

▶ Address, both physical and mailing

▶ Occupants in defendant's residence

▶ Phone numbers (home, work, cell, and pager)

- Employment history
- Educational level
- Military experience and whether discharged honorably
- Marriage
- Children and grandchildren, including names and ages
- Nature of support for the children and, if applicable, grandchildren
- Previous and present treatment for mental health issues
- Physical or mental disabilities
- Medication and medical care currently under
- Prior and present substance-addiction problems
- Prior criminal history (as discussed previously in this chapter)

It may be helpful to your practice to prepare a questionnaire that addresses these issues. I have found it much easier to ask these questions of the client myself and take my own notes regarding the answers. For whatever reason, I receive more compete answers and information this way.

Earlier in my career, I asked clients to fill out such a form. Too often, clients failed to adequately complete the form. Many criminal defense clients are not well educated and do not have the patience to complete the forms. They do not trust the criminal justice system and often will not put such information on paper in their own writing.

ADDRESS AND PHONE NUMBERS

Sometimes the defendant's physical address is relevant as it may be the actual scene of the alleged crime or be near the crime scene. Mailing address and phone numbers are necessary for maintaining contact with the client.

OCCUPANTS OF DEFENDANT'S RESIDENCE

A list of occupants and their relationship to the defendant is relevant for several reasons:

- *The defendant may still be living with the alleged victim.* This often happens in domestic dispute cases, where the alleged victim is the defendant's spouse, significant other, or relative.
- *The court may issue a restraining order on behalf of the alleged victim.* This is a court order that requires the defendant to stay away from a certain individual. Violation of the order could subject the defendant to civil contempt, bond forfeiture, and additional criminal charges for violating a restraining order. The order is often required by statute, or the court may make it a condition of the defendant's bond or conditional release. In that

case, either the defendant or the alleged victim must find a new place to live while the case is pending.

Note: You can file a motion to have a restraining order removed if the alleged victim will consent. But I have found the courts more and more reluctant to lift these restraining orders, no matter how ridiculous the charges may be, how long the couple has been together, or how many children they have together. Judges have become more sanctimonious and protective, for a lack of a better term, toward domestic violence issues. They feel as though in refusing to lift the restraining order, they are protecting the alleged victim from herself.

▶   *These individuals may be used as character witnesses or alibi witnesses.*

EMPLOYMENT

Judges are hesitant to send a working, taxpaying member of society to prison or jail. Employment is also relevant to setting the amount of bail because a working client is seen as less likely to jump bond and abscond.

EDUCATIONAL LEVEL

Educational level is relevant because the client may not be able to read or understand the documents provided. Thus, you may need to read the documents or interpret their meaning to the client.

In addition, the judge may want to know the defendant's education record when imposing conditions of a non-prison sanction. I have had many clients ordered to obtain a high school diploma or its equivalent as a condition of probation.

Education may also be relevant to the strategy of defense. It could be important in determining if the client acted or was capable of acting in accordance with a course of conduct required to commit the crime, that is, whether the defendant acted knowingly, with a particular required intent.

You may want to advise the client to earn a high school diploma or its equivalent while the case is pending in an effort to receive a more lenient sentence from the court should the defendant enter into a plea agreement or be convicted at trial.

MILITARY SERVICE

Honorable discharge from military service shows the court that the defendant can be well-disciplined. Military service is relevant to setting bail because you can argue that the defendant's success in the military shows that he will always make his court appearances and follow all bond conditions. It is relevant to sentencing because you can argue that successful completion of military service shows that the defendant can successfully complete probation or any conditions of sentence imposed upon him.

MARRIAGE AND FAMILY

A stable family relationship is a favorable sign of defendant's character. Faithfulness to a spouse and support of a family are signs of good moral character. Thus, marriage and family inquiries are relevant for mitigation in both bond and sentencing issues. Further, I have found judges less likely to send certain defendants to prison when they are the sole support for their spouse, children, or grandchildren. Some judges do not like creating wards of the state or welfare recipients by virtue of their decisions to send a defendant to prison.

A member of the family may also be a witness or codefendant to the crime. As previously discussed, there may be a restraining order forbidding contact with the alleged victim and witnesses. Also, courts issue restraining orders forbidding contact with the codefendants.

PHYSICAL AND MENTAL HEALTH

Mental health is important to the determination of the client's competence to proceed and assist with his defense. A matter cannot proceed if a defendant is mentally incompetent. If you believe that the defendant may be mentally incompetent to proceed, you must file a motion with the court requesting that the matter be removed from the docket in order to have the defendant's competency evaluated.

You can determine that a client is mentally incompetent to proceed if the client shows any sign of mental illness. For example, if the client thinks that you are George W. Bush or that the spirit of Bruce Lee lives in your diamond pendant (both have happened to me), have his competency evaluated.

The court can order an evaluation by a court-approved, neutral expert. This may involve taking the defendant into custody, if she is not already, and sending her to a state facility for testing and monitoring. (This falls under the category of a pretrial motion. This motion is addressed further in Chapter 5.) You may want to enlist the assistance of a psychological evaluator of your choosing, to avoid the lengthy, and often cumbersome, process of having the court order the evaluation.

Mental condition helps make the decision whether to use a mental disease or defect defense. If mental or physical health is a potential defense strategy issue, you may advise the defendant to have a physical or mental examination before entering into a plea agreement or sentencing.

Health can be useful evidence when arguing for a non-prison penalty or a mitigated sentence. Again, judges are hesitant to imprison the mentally ill, mentally disabled, physically disabled, or dying. Some judges simply do not want the state to have to pay for the extensive treatment that the defendant will require.

It is often useful to inform the court about the defendant's health conditions during sentencing hearing. Often, judges order defendants to work full-time as a condition of probation or other non-prison sanction. If this is the case in your jurisdiction, the judge should know if the defendant is unable to work full-time.

SUBSTANCE ABUSE

Substance-abuse issues are important because sometimes it is necessary to have the client complete a rehabilitation program prior to trial or sentencing. A defendant's voluntary submission to treatment can help with the potential penalty. (Your jurisdiction should have a list of treatment programs that are acceptable to the court.) The program will provide the defendant with proof of attendance or completion with an executed release that complies with medical privacy rules (the HIPPA law).

Judges are often pleased to see that the defendant has taken the initiative and checked himself into treatment rather than waiting for the court to order him to do so at the time of the bond hearing (some courts order the defendant into substance-abuse treatment as a condition of posting bail) or sentencing.

Substance abuse by your client is relevant to running certain defenses such as voluntary intoxication and mental incapacity. Substance abuse is often a sign of a psychiatric problem such as bipolar illness or depression. I find that many of my clients self-medicate because they have other psychological issues that have never been properly diagnosed or treated. This is true even for clients who are not charged with drug crimes. You will find an undercurrent of substance abuse in most blue-collar crimes.

A sample Client Questionnaire is included as Exhibit H on the enclosed CD-ROM. ●◆

Authority to Plea Bargain

You will have a good idea at some point during the initial interview as to whether the client wants to enter a plea agreement rather than try the case. The client often blurts out in the beginning that he does not want to take the matter to trial—he just wants you to keep him out of jail.

You must have the client's consent to approach the state regarding a plea offer. It is good to get this permission during the first meeting if the client has indicated an interest in pleading the case. This alleviates any unnecessary delay and helps to minimize legal fees and expenses.

Early plea bargaining is good for the attorney's credibility with the prosecutor. Often, the best weapon a criminal defense attorney has in his arsenal is his credibility with the prosecutor. Attempting an early resolution of a case that should probably not go to trial helps to maintain this level of credibility. (The defendant should avoid trial in a case with a legally obtained confession, several eyewitnesses, and credible physical evidence.)

In discussing plea authority you might state the following:

> Now that you have heard about the charges, the prosecution's burden of proof, the discovery, the potential penalty, and the way the process works, do you have some thought as to how you want to proceed? In other words, would you like me to pursue plea negotiations on your behalf?

If the client proclaims his innocence and demands that the matter be dismissed or go to trial, you may want to get plea negotiation authority anyway. This discussion is as follows:

> Even though you do not want to plead to anything, will you still give me permission to talk plea with the prosecutor? That will not bind you to anything; it just gives me permission to talk freely with the prosecutor. You never know, my plea discussions may lead the prosecutor to realize she has a weak case and to dismiss it. Also, although you cannot think of anything you would plead to right now, she may offer something that, at a later date, you just cannot resist. After all, you have nothing to lose by at least letting me feel the prosecutor out.

Assure the client that you will advise him of any plea offer and that you will never accept or bind him to a plea agreement without his permission. (For more discussion on the issue of plea agreements and negations, see Chapters 5 and 7.)

Validity of Evidence

In order to determine potential suppression issues (to be raised before trial by motions to suppress evidence, discussed in Chapter 5), ask the client how the evidence against him was obtained (whether a warrant to search was issued or he was taken into custody and questioned).

SEARCH

Ask if defendant's person, home, or car was searched, and whether defendant gave permission for the searches. If consent to search was given, find out if defendant was in custody when they searched his person, home, or car.

▶ A search of the person is allowed if the defendant is in custody or under arrest. Anything found through the search of defendant's person subsequent to a lawful arrest is not a violation of the Fourth Amendment.

▶ The home cannot be searched without a warrant after the defendant is in custody or under arrest, unless certain exigent circumstances exist.

▶ Likewise, unless the car is being impounded or certain exigent circumstances exist, it cannot be searched without a warrant.

STATEMENTS BY THE DEFENDANT

Ask the client if he gave a statement to the police, and where he was at the time. Was he in custody when the statement was made? Whether defendant was in custody is often determined by the totality of the circumstances. The totality of the circumstances must support the fact that the defendant was not free to leave. Consider the following circumstances:

▶ Was defendant in handcuffs?

▶ Was he in a patrol car?

▶ Was he in a police station?

▶ Was he taken somewhere away from the initial place of contact, and if so, was he free to leave?

▶ If in custody, were his rights recited to him before making any statement?

Only statements given during "custodial interrogation" are subject to suppression pursuant to *Miranda*.[4]

LEGALITY OF ARREST

Sometimes a defendant is illegally arrested. Your jurisdiction's statutes will proscribe the grounds for a lawful arrest. Any evidence obtained as a result of an unlawful arrest is subject to suppression under the Fourth Amendment.

Determine if the crime for which defendant was arrested is an arrestable offense. Some traffic offenses, petty offenses, and misdemeanor offenses are not arrestable offenses. Also, determine if there were sufficient statutory grounds to arrest the defendant for the crime alleged. If the offense is non-arrestable, the arrest is unlawful and any evidence obtained pursuant to the unlawful arrest should be suppressed.

WHAT SHOULD YOU *NOT* DO DURING THE MEETING?

▶ *Never promise the client results.* Don't guarantee that you will be able to get the case dismissed, win a suppression motion, win at trial, or get the client probation, deferred judgment (diversion), or a suspended sentence.

---

[4] In *Miranda v. Arizona*, 384 U.S. 436 (1966), the Supreme Court held that the Fifth Amendment privilege against self-incrimination (that no person "shall be compelled in any criminal case to be a witness against himself") is fully applicable during a period of "custodial interrogation."

▼ Promising the client results may assure you an invitation to speak with the disciplinary administrator, grievance board, or attorney regulation board. It is unethical to promise results.

▼ Failing your promise may expose you to civil liability. Such promises are often seen as contractual guarantees or warranties upon which the client will rely should your promised results not materialize.

▶ *Opinions about the potential for success are permissible.* You need not avoid giving the client your opinion about odds or giving your opinion as to the likelihood of certain outcomes. When my clients ask me for odds I simply tell them that criminal litigation is a "crap shoot" and that it is difficult to be certain of the ultimate outcome. Many variables play into it.

If the client continues to insist on odds, I may tell him, "The best I can give you are 50-50 odds." (The last I heard, the national defense success rate was 11 percent for outright "not guilty on all charges" verdicts at trial.[5] Quite enlightening, if you thought the O.J. Simpson, Robert Blake, and Michael Jackson verdicts represented the norm. Of note, I have met numerous attorneys with long, distinguished careers who have rarely, if ever, been successful with a motion to suppress.)

▶ *Do not confuse making promises with puffing yourself to the client.* There is nothing wrong with boasting about your abilities or successes. After all, you have got to convince the defendant to hire you. It is OK to tell the client that you believe yourself to be a good lawyer ("damn good," if you're feeling sassy). On a few occasions, I have opined that I would try the case better than the prosecutor. I follow that up with, "But even if I out-try the prosecutor, there is no guarantee that you will be acquitted."

▶ *Never speak poorly of the prosecutor, judge, or other attorneys with whom the client is consulting.* Speaking poorly of other attorneys or the judge will come back to haunt you. At some point, you can expect the client, or someone on his behalf, to reveal the bad things you have said to the person who was the subject of your insults. I learned this lesson the hard way: A client of mine wrote a judge and told her, "Although my attorney says you're a bitch, I think you are a very understanding judge."

▶ *Do not tell the client that you are close to the judge or prosecutor.* Advising the client that you have a close relationship with the court or the prosecutor may also come back to haunt you. You will regret these claims when the client tells the judge, on the record, after she has been sentenced to something more than she thought she deserved: "But Judge, my attorney told me that you and she were close." Clients usually do not comprehend the rules of ethics. Thus, it is best not to give them any rope to hang you with.

---

[5] The Western Trial Advocacy Institute, Laramie, Wyoming, July 2005.

WHAT DECISIONS SHOULD BE MADE BY THE END OF THE INITIAL MEETING (OR AT LEAST BEFORE THE PRELIMINARY HEARING)?

Whether to Proceed with the Preliminary Hearing

As discussed earlier in this chapter, the decision to have a preliminary hearing belongs exclusively to the client. Often, this decision is made during the initial meeting, but the client may need to think it over for a few days. If the client is at all hesitant about waiving the hearing, then he should be given some time to think over the decision and your advice.

Preliminary hearings are beneficial for several reasons:

▶ They enable the defense to learn the prosecutor's strategy. The prosecution's strategy is not often apparent in the charging document and the discovery.

▶ A preliminary hearing can be good trial strategy for the defense because you can box the various witnesses into certain testimony that will be beneficial to your trial strategy or theory of the case.

▶ Often, after the hearing, the prosecutor realizes he has a weak case and dismisses or makes a reasonable plea offer.

▶ Although the court may bind the matter over for trial, the court may feel that the a trial will be a waste of time and resources. Sometimes this causes future rulings to be very favorable to the defense, thus resigning the prosecutor to dismiss or extend a reasonable plea offer.

▶ After hearing how compelling the evidence is against him, the defendant may become more receptive to a plea offer.

▶ After hearing the judge rule, "I find probable cause to believe a felony has been committed, and probable cause to believe that defendant, John Doe, has committed that felony," the defendant may become more receptive to a plea offer.

Preliminary hearings are waived for any of several reasons:

▶ The defendant may want to plead to a lesser offense and resolve the matter quickly.

▶ It may be a matter of trial strategy: You do not want the prosecutor to learn the weaknesses of her case and have time to repair them before trial. (For example, your cross-examination can expose that certain scientific tests were not conducted. The prosecutor may order these tests to be conducted, and their results may be damaging to the defense.)

▶ You may want to prevent the victim or another witness from giving sworn testimony.

    ▼ The witness may disappear before trial, and you do not want his sworn testimony available to be used as a substitute.

    ▼ You do not want the witness to practice her testimony. The first time you want her to tell her story is in front of a jury. Witnesses forget and may be less helpful to the prosecution at trial.

    ▼ The witness may change her story from the statements initially made to the investigation officers. You do not want the prosecutor using the transcript of the preliminary hearing to impeach the witness should her change of story be beneficial to the defense strategy. (The prosecutor can impeach her own witness.)

▶ The preliminary hearing may be waived to avoid any further pretrial publicity. I have been surprised at how the publicity of a case diminishes by the time of the trial when the matter is not covered continuously by the press. (Ordinarily, press coverage is not favorable to the criminal defendant. You will want to avoid negative press coverage in order to prevent the jury pool from being tainted.)

(Preliminary hearing strategy is discussed more thoroughly in Chapter 3.)

Whether to Pursue an Insanity or Mental Disease or Defect Defense

The client must give permission to run this defense at trial. Most jurisdictions have a pleading or notice requirement for these types of defenses. This means that the defense must formally plead not guilty by reason of insanity either on the record or through a notice pleading that notifies the prosecution of the intent to rely upon the defense (some jurisdictions require a plea of "guilty by reason of insanity" or the like). In these jurisdictions, it is best to know during the initial meeting or sometime soon thereafter if this defense will be pursued. It may be necessary to file your notice or plead the defense before the preliminary hearing.

Note: The fact that the defendant appears to be perfectly sane at the time of the initial client meeting does not foreclose running the defense. Defendants are sometimes placed into immediate psychiatric treatment at the time of arrest. The jail administrator has broad discretion to have the defendant evaluated or treated or to pursue civil commitment proceedings for the defendant's safety and the safety of other inmates.

The prosecutor may request the court to order evaluation, treatment, or civil commitment after observing the defendant or being advised by the arresting officers of odd behavior. If the prosecutor has a reasonable belief that the defendant is not mentally competent to proceed with the case, she has an obligation to request psychiatric assistance on behalf of the defendant.

The insanity may have been temporary and manifested itself only at the time of the crime. For example, the defendant may suffer from post-traumatic stress disorder (PTSD), and was having a flashback at the time of the crime. Most people with PTSD are normal most of the time. They act out or have mental breakdowns only when they encounter certain stimuli.

Whether to Plead an Alibi

As with the insanity defense, most jurisdictions require that the alibi defense be formally pled. Often, the defense is required to disclose a list of witnesses to the alibi and their last known contact information. Therefore, a decision to run this defense should also be made during the initial meetings.

CHAPTER 3

Initial Proceedings before Trial

Having previously practiced as a civil defense lawyer, I can confidently say that criminal lawyers spend more time in court than civil lawyers do. However, criminal cases are usually resolved faster than civil cases.

Certain initial proceedings can be anticipated before a criminal trial. They include

► Advisement/First Appearance

► Appearance of Counsel

► Preliminary hearing

► Arraignment

THE FIRST APPEARANCE/ADVISEMENT

Defendant's presence in court in front of a judge or magistrate to be formally informed of the charges against him is called "The First Appearance" or "Advisement." Criminal defendants are brought before the court by a number of means, including an arrest warrant, notice to appear, or summons to appear. They may appear in custody or out of custody.

If the charge is less serious, the client may be arrested, held for a short period, and then released pending a later filing of charges. The client may be out of jail for years (depending upon the statute of limitations) until he is arrested upon a warrant for the charges or served with a notice to appear or summons to appear in court on a certain date to answer to the charges. This happens when more time is needed to investigate the case, or when the criminal court's dockets are crowded and the prosecutor does not have time to review the case and file the charging document.

At this proceeding, if no attorney is present on defendant's behalf, the defendant may be served by the court or the prosecutor with a copy of the charging document and advised by the judge of the charges against him, certain constitutional rights (which may include the right to a speedy and public trial and the right to an attorney), and the next court date.

Entry of Appearance

At the First Appearance, you will formally enter your appearance on the record, make a plea if one is requested, and ask the court to set bail if the court is open to such requests.

A formal entry of appearance is made to the judge, on the record, as follows:

> Defense Counsel: Your Honor, Mr. Defendant appears in person and through counsel, Jane Doe.

> or

> Defense Counsel: Your Honor, Jane Doe, appearing on behalf of Mr. Defendant, who appears in person and on bond (or in custody).

Thereafter, the court may ask you a few questions, including your bar number, whether you have received a copy of the charging document, whether the defendant wants a formal recitation on the record of the charges and his rights, and whether there are any additional matters to be addressed.

If the court asks you if you would like a formal recitation of the charges and rights to the defendant, answer, "No, thank you, Your Honor." This is because

▶ You should have already reviewed the charges and certain rights with the defendant during the initial meeting.

▶ Most judges get grumpy when asked to formally recite charges and rights to the defendant on the record.

▶ Asking for this makes you look ill-prepared.

If you are in fact ill-prepared, say, "Yes, thank you, Your Honor."

Addressing Bail

Bail is established by the court. It is a monetary assurance of the defendant's appearance at all future proceedings. It is an amount of money that the defendant must pay to the court in order to be released from custody until the matter is resolved.

A bail amount is not always set. Sometimes, defendants with no or a minimal criminal record will be released on their "own personal recognizance." In this situation, a defendant is released upon her assurance to the court that she will appear for every court date. Her assurance is put in writing and under oath.

Bail may not be available for some high-severity-level offenses, depending upon the jurisdiction. For instance, in Colorado, murder, kidnapping, and forcible rape are not bailable offenses. When bail is available, the judge may give the defendant the option of paying cash for the entire amount or posting a bond with the help of a professional surety (bondsman). In this situation, the defendant hires a bondsman for a certain percentage of the total bail (generally 10 to 20 percent). The bondsman gets the defendant out of jail and is responsible for his appearance in court. (Some jurisdictions require the bondsman to pay the entire amount of bail before taking the defendant out of jail.) If the defendant's bail is revoked for not appearing in court, the bondsman may be liable for the entire amount of defendant's bail set by the court. (The bondsman is usually given a certain period of time to locate the defendant and bring him to jail.)

If the defendant is in jail during the Advisement or First Appearance, ordinarily a bail has already been set. You should have determined during the initial meeting how much bail the defendant can afford to pay and, if permitted, you should ask the court to grant a bail or modify the amount of bail already imposed. For example:

> Judge: Counselors, is there anything else we need to discuss?
>
> Defense Counsel: Your Honor, are you open to discussing a bond modification at this time?
>
> Judge: Yes, counsel. You may address bond at this time.
>
> Defense Counsel: Your Honor, Mr. Defendant's bond is currently set at $15,000 cash, property, or surety. I am asking the court to reduce the bond to $1,500 cash, property, or surety. This is Mr. Defendant's first arrest for a felony charge. He is a lifelong resident of Jefferson County. He is employed full-time with Ace Management Services. He has two children, ages 7 and 11, and he has been the primary source of financial support for them for their entire lives. He will remain in the court's jurisdiction if you release him upon a lower bond. With all due respect, Your Honor, I do not think that the court took the defendant's character and ability to pay into consideration when imposing the current bond.

In some jurisdictions, the court may automatically address or readdress bond during the First Appearance, having had time to review the sworn statements supporting the arrest or charging document and the charging document itself.

Depending upon the seriousness of the charge, the court may establish or modify the bail of certain out-of-custody clients at this time. If the client cannot afford to pay the bail, he will be taken into custody.

APPEARANCE OF COUNSEL

Some jurisdictions have a proceeding that is called an Appearance of Counsel. It may take place after the First Appearance/Advisement. This is a formal proceeding in which the attorney enters an appearance to the judge, on the record. The attorney's role is essentially the same as his role in appearing at the First Appearance/Advisement, as discussed above.

THE PRELIMINARY HEARING

If the offense with which the defendant is charged is a felony, the next proceeding will be the preliminary hearing. It is an evidentiary hearing, but it is not a trial (there is never a jury). The purpose of the preliminary hearing is for the judge, after listening to evidence presented by the prosecution, to determine if there is sufficient evidence to bind the defendant over for trial—in other words, sufficient for the prosecution to keep pursuing the case against him and for a jury to decide his guilt.

The court's standard of review is to review the evidence in a light most favorable to the prosecution. The prosecution need prove to the court only that there is probable cause to believe the crime has been committed and probable cause to believe the defendant committed the crime. The defense is not required to present any evidence or argument.

The prosecution presents evidence first because the prosecution has the burden of proof. Ordinarily, the prosecutor's strategy is to put on as little evidence as possible to meet the burden of proof, because she does not want the defense to hear her whole case.

Often, the rules of evidence are relaxed at these proceedings. Many jurisdictions allow the prosecution to present its case through hearsay evidence. If your jurisdiction allows this procedure, always assume the prosecution will use only hearsay to present its case. The point of this strategy is to prevent the defendant from having access, through cross-examination, to the prosecution's witnesses. Not being able to cross-examine the witnesses keeps you from boxing them into to certain facts and contentions (which you would later use to impeach the witnesses at trial, should they deviate from their preliminary hearing testimony, or to support the defense theory of the case).

Opening Statements

Some courts will allow both sides to give an opening statement before any evidence is presented. They are sometimes waived by the lawyers because there is no jury in a preliminary hearing to persuade and because neither side wants to give away its strategy for winning the case.

Defense Counsel's Role

The defense may challenge the prosecution's evidence through cross-examination of the prosecution's witnesses, present its own evidence, and make a closing argument addressing the sufficiency of the prosecution's evidence.

CROSS-EXAMINING

It is good practice to cross-examine the state's witnesses in order to box them into certain facts. To box a witness in is to get her to testify to a certain fact that cannot be changed at a later time. If she changes her testimony at suppression motions or trial, you will use a transcript of her preliminary hearing testimony to impeach her. Box the witness into facts that are contradictory to the prosecution's theory of the case and helpful to the defense theory of the case.

Leading questions can help box the witness in to a certain fact. For example, part of this defense strategy was that because it was dark out, the eyewitnesses really could not see who was the aggressor and what happened during the assault, supporting the theory that defendant acted in self-defense.

> Defense Counsel: Mr. Witness, I want to speak to you about the time of day this crime occurred.
>
> Witness: Okay.
>
> Defense Counsel: You told Officer Story that it was dark out at the time of the fight in the alley, did you not?
>
> Witness: I believe so.
>
> Defense Counsel: You also told him that because of the dark, it was hard to see what was going on in the alley, did you not?
>
> Witness: That's true.

In general, you should avoid questions that will bring out certain facts unhelpful to the defense strategy or theory. If, however, there is no other way to explore these facts with the witness, e.g., through an interview with the witness and defense investigator at a later time, it is best to learn now, before the trial, all of the bad things about which the witness could testify. That way, the defense can develop an explanation, response, or contradiction in order to explain them away at trial.

Open-ended questions are sometimes the best way to get as much information as possible. Open-ended questions are questions that do not suggest the answer to the witness and are questions that you do not know how the witness will answer. For example, if my defendant is charged with assault and the police reports state that the alleged victim was at a bar earlier that evening but provide no other details, I want to know all about this bar, including whether the victim was drinking, how much she was drinking, whether she was with other people, how much they were drinking, and so forth. In questioning the alleged victim during the preliminary hearing, I may find some golden nuggets that may help me impeach her credibility or recollection at trial.

My defense theory is that the victim was heavily intoxicated, that she swung at the defendant, that defendant pushed her to get her away and off of him, and that she fell and hurt herself because she was intoxicated. (This is a classic case of justifiable self-defense.) I begin my cross-examination of the alleged victim with an open-ended question, in the hopes of learning that she was antagonizing my client before the alleged assault or doing something she probably was not supposed to be doing.

> Defense Counsel: What had you been doing right before you say the defendant came over to you and started yelling?
>
> Witness: Well, we had been inside the Whiskey Tango bar hanging out.
>
> Defense Counsel: Who is "we"? [Up to this point, I was not aware that the alleged victim was with anyone else that night.]
>
> Witness: Ugh, Amy Mattingly, John Brown, Lizzie Borden, Paul Bunion, and some guy named Rick.
>
> Defense Counsel: Are any of these individuals related to you? [Relation may show a witness's bias.]
>
> Witness: Yeah, Amy's my sister and Paul is my cousin.
>
> Defense Counsel: This guy named Rick. Did you see who he was there with?
>
> Witness: Yeah, he came with my friend Lizzie.
>
> Defense Counsel: Your friend Lizzie Borden?
>
> Witness: Yeah.
>
> Defense Counsel: Now when you say you were "hanging out" at this bar, what does that mean?
>
> Witness: We were having a couple of drinks and talking.
>
> Defense Counsel: Was everybody you were with having a couple of drinks?
>
> Witness: Yeah.
>
> Defense Counsel: How many drinks did you have?
>
> Witness: About four drinks.
>
> Defense Counsel: Did you count or are you guessing?
>
> Witness: Well, I drank a pitcher of beer by myself, and that's usually about four glasses.
>
> Defense Counsel: How tall are you?
>
> Witness: About 5'1".

Defense Counsel: How much do you weigh?

Witness: About 115.

Defense Counsel: How long were you in the bar?

Witness: About an hour and a half.

I just hit a gold mine. I have found out from the alleged victim herself that she and her friends were drinking. In addition, I found out enough information to argue to the jury that she was intoxicated. A 5'1", 115-pound woman is ordinarily going to be intoxicated after drinking a pitcher of beer in approximately an hour and a half.

PRESENTING DEFENSE EVIDENCE

After the prosecution has rested, the defense may be given an opportunity to present any relevant evidence through witness testimony. Some courts, after listening to the prosecution's evidence, disallow defense evidence altogether at the preliminary hearing. Still other courts will not let the defense's evidence duplicate evidence presented by the prosecution. Most courts limit the defense's ability to present witness testimony and often will not allow the defense to call witnesses to testify to matters outside the scope of the matters testified to by the prosecution witnesses. Although the defendant may testify, if she does so she waives her Fifth Amendment right to remain silent. Thus, I cannot envision a scenario where it would be wise to call the defendant as a witness.

As discussed earlier, I have never called witnesses to testify at the preliminary hearing. The burden of proof upon the prosecution is so low that in nearly every case, if the prosecutor presents some evidence regarding each necessary element of the crimes charged, the defendant will be bound over for trial. Thus, I find no need to give the state an opportunity to figure out the defense case strategy by presenting evidence or witnesses. Just as the prosecutor desires to limit my access to its witnesses before trial, I too do not want the prosecutor to have access to my witnesses before trial.

Waiving the Preliminary Hearing

Sometimes it is necessary or desirable to waive the preliminary hearing. Some common reasons:

▶ The possibility that evidence presented at the hearing will result in additional charges. For example, a defendant is charged with one count of sexual assault, but the evidence at preliminary hearing will reveal that the victim claims the defendant assaulted her three times during the incident. Each assault is a separate crime. Therefore, the prosecutor may add two additional charges of assault.

▶ To waive the preliminary hearing in exchange for a plea offer. Sometimes prosecutors will make a plea offer and leave it open for discussion if the defendant will waive his preliminary hearing.

▶ The evidence is so overwhelming against the defendant that a preliminary hearing would be an unnecessary waste of the prosecutor's time. In that event, the defendant waives in order to stay in the prosecutor's good graces in hopes for a reasonable plea offer at a later date.

▶ If the case is high profile, to avoid media pretrial coverage and disclosure of certain facts to the public. Preliminary hearings are ordinarily open to the public, including the press.

▶ To keep the prosecution from having preliminary hearing testimony on the record in the event a prosecution witness does not appear at trial. If there is no preliminary hearing, there is no transcript of testimony that the prosecution can ask to be read into evidence; any other statements made by the missing witness are inadmissible hearsay at trial.

When waiving the hearing, some judges make a record indicating that the defendant desires to waive his right to the preliminary hearing. An example transcript of this proceeding follows:

> Judge: The court calls case number 04CR1987. The court notes that both counsel and the defendant are present. The court has been advised off the record that the defendant desires to waive his right to a preliminary hearing. Is that correct, counsel?
>
> Defense Counsel: Yes, Your Honor.
>
> Judge: Is that correct, Mr. Defendant?
>
> Defendant: Yes, Your Honor.
>
> Judge: Very well, the court accepts defendant's waiver and binds this matter over for trial. The court sets arraignment for November 14, 2007, at 8:00 a.m. in this division. Thank you, counsel, any other matters to address at this time?
>
> Defense Counsel: No, Your Honor. Thank you.
>
> Prosecutor: No, Your Honor.

Other courts require the attorney and client to make certain formal representations about the waiver on the record. An example transcript of a formal waiver is as follows:

> Judge: The court calls case number 04CR1987. Can I have appearances of counsel, please.
>
> Defense Counsel: Your Honor, Mr. Defendant appears in person and through counsel, Jane Doe.

Prosecutor: Your Honor, Dewey Cheatum appears on behalf of the State.

Judge: This matter comes on the docket for preliminary hearing this afternoon. How would the parties like to proceed?

Defense Counsel: Your Honor, the defendant desires to waive his preliminary hearing at this time.

Judge: Mr. Defendant, I have been advised by your counsel that you wish to waive your right to a preliminary hearing. Is that correct?

Defendant: Yes, Your Honor.

Judge: Well, Mr. Defendant, do you understand that by waiving your right to a preliminary hearing, I will make a finding, without hearing any evidence, that there is probable cause to believe that the felony in the complaint was committed and probable cause to believe that you committed that felony and you will be bound over for trial?

Defendant: Yes, Your Honor.

Judge: Understanding your right to a preliminary hearing, is it your desire here today to waive your right to a preliminary hearing?

Defendant: Yes, Your Honor.

Judge: Very well, I will make a probable cause finding that the felony in the complaint has been committed and a probable cause finding to believe that Mr. Defendant committed that felony described therein and bind him over for trial of this matter.

A sample Preliminary Hearing Waiver/Order is attached as Exhibit I. ●◆

THE ARRAIGNMENT

The arraignment is a proceeding in which the defendant is formally advised of his charges and enters a formal plea, and a trial date is set (or a pretrial conference is scheduled to set a trial date). Sometimes the arraignment is held immediately after the preliminary hearing; otherwise, a later date and time are scheduled.

There are usually three types of pleas that can be made by the defendant at the arraignment: guilty, not guilty, or stands mute. The "stands mute" plea is pursued if the defense believes that there is a flaw in the charging document (which is a challenge to jurisdiction) or that the court lacks jurisdiction on other grounds. Ordinarily, the defendant waives the right to challenge jurisdiction if he makes a formal plea at the arraignment. Therefore, the benefit to standing mute is that it preserves the right to challenge the court's jurisdiction.

If the defendant stands mute as to plea, the court will enter a plea of "not guilty" on the defendant's behalf.

The following is an example of a formal arraignment:

Judge: Counsel, may we proceed to arraignment?

Defense Counsel: Yes, Your Honor. We acknowledge receipt of the complaint and information, waive formal reading of this document and further advisement of rights, enter a plea of not guilty, and request the matter be set for a jury trial.

Judge: Very well, the court sets trial for [time and date].

An example of a formal arraignment wherein the defendant stands mute as to plea is as follows:

Judge: Counsel, may we proceed to arraignment?

Defense Counsel: Yes, Your Honor. We acknowledge receipt of the complaint and information, waive formal reading of this document, and stand mute as to plea.

Judge: Very well, the court will enter a plea of "not guilty" on the defendant's behalf. Are there any other matters that need to be taken up at this time?

Defense Counsel: May it please the court, having had a plea formally entered by the court, the defendant requests a jury trial at this time.

TIPS FOR THE ARRAIGNMENT

1. Always read the copy of the charging document upon which defendant is arraigned. Mistakes or typos regarding time, date, venue, and the crime charged can be fatal flaws for the prosecution. They may cause the court to lack jurisdiction of the matter. If you believe the court may lack jurisdiction, the defendant should stand mute as to plea.

    ▶ In addition, the original charges may have changed since the preliminary hearing or new charges may have been added without your knowledge between the preliminary hearing and the arraignment. It is important to catch these early, because the changes or additions give the defendant a right to a new preliminary hearing (even if he waived his original preliminary hearing).

2. Always request a jury trial. Some courts hold that if a formal request for a jury trial is not made on the record at the arraignment, the jury trial is waived and the matter must be tried to the court.

▶ A jury trial is almost always preferable to a bench trial. In a jury trial, the prosecution must convince six to 12 individuals of the defendant's guilt, as opposed to convincing one often cynical judge. Thus your client's odds are better with a jury trial.

▶ The only time to try the issue to the court is when the case comes down to a complex legal issue and the facts are not much contested. For instance, I once tried a DUI and voluntary manslaughter to the court because the key issue was whether or not the defendant's actions in driving under the influence was the proximate cause of the pedestrian victim's death. (Much like the tort of negligence, most jurisdictions require that in a homicide, the defendant's conduct must have proximately caused the victim's death.) The defense claimed that the victim, by his own negligence, was the proximate cause of his own death. The victim was walking in the road, at night, in a poorly lit area, and he was wearing dark clothing and a camouflage jacket. We tried the matter to the court because we did not trust the jury to understand the law regarding proximate causation.

3. There is rarely a time that the defendant will plead guilty at the arraignment (except if perhaps the arraignment and plea agreement hearing are held at the same time). I frankly question why pleading guilty is even an option at the arraignment. Even if the defendant hopes for a plea offer from the prosecutor, he must plead "not guilty" to preserve his constitutional right to a trial. This is necessary should the court reject his subsequent plea.

CHAPTER 4

Pretrial Communication
with the Prosecutor and the Court

COMMUNICATING WITH THE PROSECUTOR

I find the following to be helpful in dealing with prosecutors.

Know the Facts Better Than the Prosecutor Does

A competent grasp of the facts tells the prosecutor that you know what you are doing and that the prosecutor will have to spend more time than usual prepping the case for hearing or trial. I have found that some prosecutors are quite lazy in their pretrial preparation. They wait until the very last minute to prepare their case or to develop a thorough understanding of the facts. Thus, if the prosecutor perceives a long, exhaustive preparation ahead, she may be willing to give more when negotiating.

Note: Never give away your entire defense or theory of the case during these discussions. You do not want the negotiations to fall through and then be left with the prosecutor knowing your entire defense strategy. If you have to draw on the facts of the case during negotiations, rely on the undisputed facts.

There is no bright line as to how much information you should reveal. Use your best judgment, which should include your impression of the prosecutor's intelligence level and the possibilities that he will use any revelations to the defense's disadvantage during trial or pretrial motions. For instance, if you are contesting not that a victim was assaulted but only that your client was involved, it is OK to tell the prosecutor that your client did not do it. It is probably OK to say somebody else did it. That doesn't really give away your strategy. You may, however, draw the line at telling the prosecutor who you think did it, if you know. After all, you do not want the prosecutor spending all of his trial preparation before trial precluding every possibility that the individual you named was involved.

However, it is OK to focus on the obvious facts bad for the prosecution's case. For example:

▶ "Mr. Prosecutor, you have no fingerprint evidence tying the defendant to the weapon found at the scene."

▶ "Mr. Prosecutor, your ballistics report is inconclusive."

▶ "Mr. Prosecutor, your arresting officer, Officer Unfriendly, was suspended from the force last month for lying on the stand."

▶ "Mr. Prosecutor, your lead investigator did not even attempt to have the evidence tested for DNA."

Be Polite

Many criminal defense lawyers perceive the prosecutor as the enemy. While you should not think of the prosecutor as your friend, rudeness or hostility will only hurt you and your client.

Prosecutors despise rude and arrogant defense attorneys and look forward to taking them to court whenever possible. I have watched many attorneys damage their clients by their rude behavior toward the prosecution. In these instances, the prosecutors have refused to give the clients a reasonable plea offer or refused what would ordinarily be reasonable discovery requests or bond proposals out of disdain for the attorneys. It may be unethical, but it happens.

The more pleasant you are, the more difficult it is for the prosecutor to be rude to you. And, in time, your pleasant demeanor will help you to build a good rapport with certain prosecutors and they will be willing to give more when negotiating certain matters of the case. Besides trial skills, being respected and having a good reputation are usually the most valuable negotiation tools the criminal defense attorney has.

Even if the prosecutor is rude and virtually unbearable, keep your cool. Doing so throws them off balance. When the prosecutor is off balance, the defense attorney has the upper hand—especially at trial.

As a new attorney in the jurisdiction, expect that many prosecutors (and some judges) will be rude or condescending to you in your initial dealings. Do not take it personally and do not respond in kind.

Choose Your Battles

Choose your battles wisely. The inability to pick a battle has been the demise of many good attorneys. You must determine if a case is a possible winner, a "dead-bang loser," or has 50-50 odds with the right jury panel (I usually envision that panel to consist of ten people who believe in alien abduction and a Hoover or Johnson conspiracy to assassinate President Kennedy).

Once you have a good grasp of the facts and discovery of the case, you should determine the case's winnability. Trial experience will inevitably help develop this skill. To that end, I look upon every trial as a beneficial learning experience (no matter how badly I may get beaten).

Your approach to the prosecutor should be governed by your evaluation of the case. Your approach should be more humbled when you are dealing with a dead-bang-loser case. In other words, avoid touting the winnability of the case or making assurances about the veracity of certain evidence when you are really praying for the best resolution possible for your client. For example, if the case involves a clear confession, physical evidence tying the client to the crime, several eyewitnesses identifying the client, and a video of the client committing the crime, you should probably avoid approaching the prosecutor and telling him that he must dismiss the case or else, especially if your goal is merely to have your client serve as little time as possible. That case is probably what I call a dead-bang loser, and your dealings with the prosecutor should be tempered by this fact. You lose credibility in situations in which you approach negotiations and discussions with unrealistic expectations. Approach the prosecutor with hat in hand as opposed to ready to fight (or, as they say in Kansas, "with your gun loaded for bear").

I am not saying that you should avoid zealously defending your obviously guilty client. But as a criminal defense attorney, your credibility is often the only ammunition you have. Your credibility as an attorney helps the client who has a dead-bang–loser case as well because credible and respected attorneys get better plea bargain offers.

Regardless of your case assessment, avoid battling over every single point. Pick those points that are material, relevant, and worthy of the fight. When an issue is trivial and collateral, and winning it will not give the defense a strategic benefit, it may be wise to give it up. For example, when you have a great suppression or limine issue, do not waste precious time and credibility fighting over the fact that the prosecutor sent you the investigation officer's field notes (handwritten notes taken during the investigation) two days after the discovery deadline has passed—especially when you have had the investigator's official report all along.

If you battle over every little point, you will not only lose favor with the prosecutor, but you will start a vicious war in which the prosecutor will thereafter fight you over every little point of contention. The prosecution has all the money and resources—they are the government and often have huge taxpayer-financed war chests, or at the very least, a bigger war chest than you (unless your client is a high-paid professional basketball player). The prosecutor, if she has any intelligence, will always have the means to wear you down, take you offsides, and make you lose sight of your defense strategy.

Never Lie

Do not lie about a fact, a witness, the law, or anything else when dealing with the prosecutor (or the court). Not only is it unethical, but lying causes you to lose all credibility with the prosecutor and his colleagues.

I cannot state this enough: Once your credibility is lost, you will lose respect and potential favorable treatment, thereby losing any advantage you may have had on behalf of your client. Good lawyers do not lie, or ever find themselves in any situation that would call for lying.

Dealing with the Evil, Lying Prosecutor

Please do not confuse my advice thus far for adoration of the prosecution. I have had many tussles with evil, vile, untrustworthy prosecutors—and I couldn't care less if I ever have good standing or credibility with them. About 5 to 10 percent of prosecutors fall into this category, and you will know them when you see them: They hide discovery, lie to you, and lie to the court about representations you have made or never made and so on.

Once these people have betrayed your trust, they have no credibility and you may treat them accordingly. Should you be betrayed by them a second time, it is your fault as you should have known better.

TIPS FOR DEALING WITH A HOSTILE PROSECUTOR

1. Tell the prosecutor in a professional letter that, due to the difficulties you have been having in resolving your differences, you will communicate only in writing. A sample Letter to Prosecutor is included as Exhibit J on the enclosed CD-ROM. •◦

2. If appropriate, and not detrimental to your client's case, send the prosecutor letters or e-mails as often as possible so that if it becomes relevant to the court you can show that you zealously kept open the lines of communication.

3. Always keep copies of your letters and e-mails to and from the prosecutor. If necessary, you can mark them as exhibits and attach them to motions or enter them into the record at hearings to prove to the judge that

   ▼ The prosecutor is making false representations to the court, or

   ▼ The prosecutor is deserving of sanctions for avoiding your numerous requests for discoverable material.

4. As a last resort, if your personal dislike of the prosecutor consumes your attention, you may need to sit down with the client or the judge and suggest that a new attorney get involved.

5. Never let your personal feelings get in the way of effectively representing the client.

COMMUNICATING WITH THE COURT

Some judges become cynical, and sometimes jaded, after many years on the bench. That being the case, the new criminal defense attorney should assume that his client may be viewed suspiciously by the court.

For this reason, always strive to behave more professionally than the prosecutors do. The attorney who has the court's respect is more likely to have the court's attention and, therefore, can more effectively represent the client's rights.

TIPS FOR COMMUNICATING WITH THE COURT

1. *Introduce yourself.* There is nothing worse than being in the middle of a motion and having the judge call out, "Who are you? Have you ever been in my court before?" That is among the last things your client wants to hear from the court. Always introduce yourself to the judge in chambers and, if possible, before court begins. It shows respect for the judge and sends a message that you are a professional, respectful lawyer.

   ▼ Do not talk about the case that brings you before the court.

   ▼ Say, "Your Honor, I am Joe Lawyer. I am here today regarding the John Defendant matter. I had never formally met you and thought I would introduce myself before I appeared in front of you. It is a pleasure to meet you, Your Honor."

2. *Learn the judge's likes and dislikes.* When introducing yourself, ask the judge her likes and dislikes about courtroom behavior. As an example, some judges allow attorneys to have a glass of water or coffee in the courtroom during hearings, while the same conduct will get you ejected from other judges' courtrooms.

   ▼ I like to approach the judge and ask the following, "Judge, since I have never practiced in your courtroom before, is there anything you would like me to know about your courtroom rules or preferences?"

   ▼ If the judge is not available, ask her administrative assistant, law clerk, and court reporter. They have a lot of information about the judge's personal preferences.

3. *Be kind to the judge's assistants.* Always treat the judge's assistants with respect, professionalism, and kindness.

   ▼ Nice attorneys have an "in" to the judge's chambers through his staff.

   ▼ The court staff runs the show. They often know more about what is going on the chambers than the judge does. Essentially, the court's assistants hold the keys to the kingdom.

▼ Kindness and courtesy will get you far when asking for hearing dates, asking to be allowed to have your hearing bumped to the beginning of the docket to accommodate your schedule, or asking for a last-minute hearing transcript (should the judge have his own court reporter).

▼ Your rapport with the judge often depends upon your rapport with his staff. If they do not like you, you can be assured that the judge will hear about it.

▼ Likewise, the judge's treatment of you is often governed by how well his staff likes you.

4. *Avoid ex parte communication.* Ex parte communication is communication with the judge outside the presence of opposing counsel.

▼ As a general rule, it unethical to speak to a judge about any matter that is before her without the presence of opposing counsel.

▼ If you do approach a judge and ask to speak with her about a matter that is before her, make certain that you have permission from the prosecutor and you advise the judge of that fact before she gives you permission to discuss the matter with her.

5. *Always be punctual.* Timeliness is seen by the court as respect.

▼ Appear to any court matter on time or early.

▼ Try to arrive early at all hearings before the prosecutor. Being early can boost your confidence that you are more prepared than the other side.

▼ Let the judge see that you are early. It sends a message that you are respectful and prepared.

▼ If you are running a little late, call the judge's chambers or stop by his chambers in advance and advise the court staff of your situation and assure them that you will appear as soon as you are able.

▼ If you were late, stay after your hearing and make a humble apology to the judge in chambers and assure him that your tardiness was out of the ordinary, if you are able. This will not be seen as ex parte communication.

▼ If you are late the first time you appear in front of a particular judge, you can be assured that you have started out on the wrong foot. I was late for my first appearance ever in front of a certain district court judge. He never forgave me. He was one of those judges that almost everyone in the defense bar liked and respected. But he disliked me and would often let me know it, without coming right out and saying so. I received a lot of unfavorable rulings from him, rulings that shocked and surprised my defense colleagues when I described them.

They would say, "Judge Voldemort would never do that to me. Are you sure we're talking about the same judge?" Fortunately for my clients, I eventually moved out of his jurisdiction.

6. *Promptly return all calls and letters.*

   ▼ If the judge is calling or writing, always assume it is important.

   ▼ Prompt means as soon as you return to the office or receive the message. Do not postpone until tomorrow or the next day.

   ▼ Your prompt response is a matter of respect and professional courtesy.

7. *Always be prepared.* When you appear in court, be prepared to argue the issue at hand and any collateral issues dealing with your case. I once had a pretrial hearing wherein the judge asked the prosecutor a question about a matter that was certainly germane to the issue at hand and she responded, "I am not prepared to argue that issue today." I am confident that the judge told her supervisor because she was not employed for very long after that.

   ▼ Know your case. Know your theory of the case and the facts that support it.

   ▼ Be prepared to respond to any argument adverse to your position on any issue.

   ▼ Know the statutes (ordinances) and relevant caselaw, and if helpful, have copies available for the court and opposing counsel.

   ▼ An attorney looks incompetent and loses the court's respect if she has to ask for a break to find a statute or case; further, she will probably not get it.

8. *Always address the court formally.* Whether you are in the courtroom, in chambers or outside of the courthouse, always address the judge with, "Your Honor" or "Judge." Never address a female judge as "Ma'am."

9. *Use the courtroom podium and other furniture properly.* Misuse of the podium and courtroom furniture is very disrespectful, and some judges will not hesitate to point that out to you in a crowded courtroom. Additionally, it makes you look sloppy.

   ▼ If the courtroom has a podium, assume that the judge wants you to use it. Use it properly; do not lean on it, put your feet on it, or stand on it (with one foot or two feet). Believe me, this really happens.

   ▼ Likewise, do not allow your client to lean or stand on the podium.

   ▼ If you desire to address the judge from a courtroom table, ask the judge for permission before beginning your presentation.

10. *Always stand when addressing the court.* Unless otherwise instructed, you should always stand when addressing the judge. Lifting your behind about six inches from your chair when making a quick announcement or answering a quick question does not constitute standing. This quick-lift is a bad habit that many prosecutors have embraced. Many judges find it disrespectful, and it is disrespectful to the jury. It not only looks sloppy, it impedes your ability to properly project and inflect your voice.

11. *Never lie or make assumptions to the court.*

   ▼ It is better to be in trouble with the court for not following procedure than lying to the court about it. If you are caught lying, you will never be considered credible by the court.

   ▼ Lying is unethical and is grounds for suspension or disbarment.

   ▼ Never make representations that you merely assume. For example, if you think your investigator or process server has served process on a witness, but you are not certain, do not advise the court that you have served the witness with process. If it is later discovered by the court that you did not have service, the judge may assume that you were dishonest.

   ▼ Although responding to a court inquiry with "I don't know" is not flattering, it is received better than a lie or reckless assumption.

   ▼ Be careful not to get caught up in repeating your client's lie to the court. You will lose credibility with the judge if you blindly repeat to the court a client's statement that later turns out to be false. Because clients sometimes lie, when you make representations to the court about something a client has told you, say your client has "advised" you; for example, "Your Honor, Mr. Defendant has advised me that he has completed drug treatment." A more definitive statement may make the judge feel that you are complicit in the client's lie.

   I learned this lesson the hard way. I once advised a judge that my client had finished drug treatment at a particular program. I did so because the client had assured me. The judge had a phone at the bench and proceeded to call the treatment center. I was surprised and humiliated when the judge was informed by the treatment center that my client had been unsuccessfully discharged from the program for nonattendance. I later found myself cowering in chambers asking humbly for the judge's forgiveness for my statement. The judge was disappointed in me and advised me to be more careful with my client's representations to the court.

12. *Pick your battles.* As with dealing with the prosecutor, pick your battles on issues before the court.

▼ If you fight for every little issue that a judge could consider trivial or collateral, you may lose credibility with the court. This will undermine any legitimate motions you may file in the future.

▼ With some courts, it is best to attempt to resolve a matter outside the presence of the court before filing a motion or bringing the matter before the court. Judges appreciate this because it helps them to better manage their dockets. Many require it.

▼ Try to avoid filing canned or form motions. These are motions that are specific to a certain issue. The attorney merely changes the defendant's name and case number in the motion's caption and does not tailor the language of the motion to the specific facts and circumstances of the case. (You can find form motions in many practice and procedure compendiums in your firm's brief library, or you may write your own.) The more of these motions you file, the more likely that a judge will discount your future motions—even when they are not canned.

13. *Be respectful outside of the court and chambers.* Judges are humans too and they have outside lives just like the rest of us. You will run into judges on the street. When you do, address them with respect. You do not have to avoid them.

▼ Casual conversations outside of the courthouse with the judge are entirely appropriate so long as you do not discuss matters before the court.

▼ I like to wave at judges and, if possible, approach and say "hello." I may make small talk, such as, "How about those Broncos?"

▼ It is always a good thing to engage the judge outside of the courtroom and get to know him personally.

▼ If a judge respects you personally, she is more likely to respect you in the courtroom.

CHAPTER 5

General Pretrial Pleading and Motion Practice

The following are generally accepted and used pretrial pleadings and motions.

ENTRY OF APPEARANCE

An Entry of Appearance notifies the world that you are the defendant's attorney and provides your contact information. This is a pleading filed by the defense attorney when first retained on the case. Many courts require them.

After the Entry of Appearance is filed, the court and the prosecutor will notify you directly as to any matter regarding the case.

A sample Entry of Appearance is included as Exhibit K on the enclosed CD-ROM. ➥

NOTICE OR REQUEST FOR JURY TRIAL

Ordinarily, a jury trial is orally requested on the record at arraignment. However, some jurisdictions (e.g., municipal courts and county courts) often require a written request for a jury trial.

The deadline to file your written notice is specified by statute or code. Should you fail to file the request by the required date, the defendant will not be entitled to a jury trial. His matter will instead be tried to a judge. (This is because jury trials can be costly to the municipality and take up more of the court's time than bench trials.)

A jury trial is usually better for your client than a bench trial because in a jury trial the prosecution must convince six to 12 individuals of the defendant's guilt rather than just one judge. (The number of jurors is also prescribed by statute or code.) This increases your odds of acquittal. Another drawback to a bench trial is that judges can be cynical and unwilling to listen to your defense theory. (This issue is discussed in Chapter 4.)

A sample Request for Jury Trial is included as Exhibit L on the enclosed CD-ROM. ➦

MOTION TO MODIFY BAIL OR BOND

If the defendant retains you while she is in custody, it may be necessary to file a motion to modify bail. This is a motion stating that the bail or bond set exceeds the defendant's ability to pay and requesting that it be reduced.

The motion should include the following:

▶ The nature of the charge

▶ The amount of bond/bail previously set

▶ A request for a reduction of that bail/bond

▶ A simple statement that advises the court of the address at which the defendant will be staying should she be released on a lower bond

▶ If necessary, an indication that the defendant will remain within the court's jurisdiction awaiting trial of the matter.

Requests that the defendant be released on her personal recognizance (PR bond) or her own recognizance (OR bond) should be handled in the same manner. These types of bonds allow the defendant to sign a document swearing that she will appear timely at all court proceedings involved with the case. These bonds enable the defendant to be released without paying any bail money, though they may designate a sum of money that the defendant will have to pay should she violate the bond by failing to appear in court.

The court has broad discretion in addressing bail and may take into account the following:

▶ The nature of the crime

▶ The weight of the evidence

▶ Family ties

▶ Employment

▶ Financial resources

▶ Character and mental condition

▶ Community ties

▶ Prior convictions

▶ Prior failures to appear in court

▶   Prior bond forfeitures

A sample Motion to Modify Bond is included as Exhibit M on the enclosed CD-ROM. ➛

DISCOVERY MOTIONS

Discovery motions are filed in order to ensure that you receive (or be allowed to review) all relevant evidence in the control of the prosecutor.

As discussed in Chapters 1 and 2, such motions are not always necessary. If you have entered your appearance (on the record in open court or by filing a written Entry of Appearance), the prosecutor owes you discovery, without a formal order from the court forcing him to reveal the evidence collected to date. Often before filing such motions I first make an informal request to the prosecutor by phone or by letter (documenting the request with a memo to the file or a copy of the letter placed in the file).

Sometimes, after reviewing the discovery provided, I file a motion for discovery requesting the prosecutor to produce specific items that I learn about from discovery materials I did receive. For instance, if I am provided a transcript of an interview, but no cassette, VHS tape, or DVD containing the actual interview transcribed, then I may file the motion and make a formal request for the recording itself. Transcripts of recorded interviews are compiled by the police department or the prosecution. Always compare the transcript to the original recording. Transcripts often contain errors that can be detrimental to your case.

Often, prosecutors do not know what they have or what information is still in the custody of their investigating officers. You may have to be persistent with them, by filing motions for discovery, in order to obtain or review every piece of relevant information.

A sample Motion for Discovery is included as Exhibit N on the enclosed CD-ROM. ➛

MOTION TO COMPEL DISCOVERY

Motions to compel discovery are filed with the court after you have exhausted all other methods of getting the prosecutor to produce the relevant information you want.

If the prosecutor fails to abide by the court's order granting your motion to compel discovery, then you may be entitled to file a motion requesting sanctions, which may include

▶ Preventing the prosecutor from putting on certain evidence at trial

▶ Dismissal of the charges (which is a rare sanction imposed by courts only after egregious behavior by the prosecutor).

A sample Motion to Compel Discovery is included as Exhibit O on the enclosed CD-ROM. ➥

MOTION TO TAKE DEPOSITION

Some jurisdictions allow you to depose certain witnesses in anticipation of trial. Unlike civil depositions, you often need permission from the court to take them. Thus, you may need to file a motion to take deposition.

Set out in your motion the need to have a certain witness testify on the record. Grounds supporting such a motion include

▶ The witness to be deposed will be leaving the court's subpoena jurisdiction

▶ Defense counsel is concerned that the witness will not make himself available to testify at trial

In most jurisdictions that require a court order to take a deposition, the deposition will be taken in the courtroom and will be presided over by a judge. (Civil depositions are not taken in the courtroom and do not involve a presiding judge.)

A sample Motion to Take Deposition is included as Exhibit P on the enclosed CD-ROM. ➥

MOTION FOR PSYCHOLOGICAL OR PHYSICAL EXAMINATION

An evaluation of the alleged victim's mental or physical health may be helpful to the defense strategy. Often, the prosecutor or police will send an alleged sexual-assault victim to a psychologist who may then testify for the prosecution that the victim exhibits psychological symptoms consistent with a victim of sexual assault. An evaluation by a psychological expert hired by the defense may contradict the prosecutor's psychological expert. The field of forensic psychology has developed several standardized tests to determine if the test-taker is actually suffering from a psychological condition or is exaggerating her symptoms.

In cases where serious bodily injury or permanent disfigurement to the victim is alleged by the prosecution as an element of the crime charged or as a sentence enhancer, an evaluation by a physician (one specializing in emergency medicine, rehabilitation medicine, or trauma surgery) hired by the defense may contradict these allegations.

A court order is required in order to have a victim or a witness analyzed by a psychological expert or a physician. These motions can be difficult to win, as judges may consider them invasive and often require that you provide proof of a prior condition of the victim or witness that makes the psychological or physical examination relevant. Mere hearsay, a hunch, or even an indication in the discovery provided by the prosecution about prior mental or physical conditions are usually not enough to justify the court granting such an order.

Do not despair if the court denies your request for an examination. You can still hire an expert to review the prosecution expert's report. Your expert may be able to testify that the prosecution's expert is wrong or failed to follow certain protocols. Your expert may assist you in preparing your cross-examination of the prosecution's expert (e.g., educate you in the area or provide you with various learned treatises that may be used to impeach the prosecution expert on cross-examination).

A sample Motion for Psychological Evaluation is included as Exhibit Q on the enclosed CD-ROM. ••

MOTION TO DETERMINE DEFENDANT'S COMPETENCY TO STAND TRIAL

A defendant must be competent in order to proceed to trial. The right to be tried while competent is protected by due process of the law. If the defendant is not competent, a motion to determine competency should be filed.

► A defendant is not competent if he is unable to understand the charge against him or the potential consequences that a conviction may bring.

► A defendant is not competent if he cannot assist his attorney in his defense.

An incompetent defendant will not volunteer to you that he is incompetent. Therefore, you should file a competency motion when he exhibits any sort of odd behavior that leads you to question his mental stability, such as having to consult with some invisible person in the room before answering your questions, or attempting suicide since being charged.

In the motion, you request that the defendant's case be taken out of the docket rotation and that all future proceedings be suspended until the defendant is rendered competent by the appropriate authorities supported by statute. Unless the court demands specific incidents, put in your motion and argue at hearing only that you have a good faith basis to believe your client is not competent to proceed as he cannot assist you in his defense. If your client has confided in you that he is the President of the United States, that conversation is protected by the attorney–client privilege and you are not required to divulge that conversation to the court.

If granted, the client's right to a speedy trial is suspended until the matter is placed back on the docket. After the hearing, the court will order the client to be evaluated by a court-authorized expert and a report will be made to the court about the defendant's competency.

If the defendant is deemed incompetent, he will be treated or institutionalized until he is determined by an authorized evaluator to be competent to stand trial. Some defendants are never found to be competent to stand trial; in these cases, the prosecution often initiates civil commitment proceedings.

Do not confuse competency motions with an insanity defense. You can present an insanity defense and still have a client who is competent to stand trial. As a matter of fact, the client must be competent, and be able to assist with his defense, in order to be able to run such a defense.

A sample Competency Motion is included as Exhibit R on the enclosed CD-ROM. ➥

MOTION FOR A BILL OF PARTICULARS

A motion for a bill of particulars sets out your specific concerns or the vague attributes of the charging document and requests that the court order the prosecutor to provide a bill of particulars identifying in more detail the facts that form the basis for the charge.

For instance, if the client is charged with rape, but the facts that form the basis for the rape are unclear from the charging document (e.g., whether he is being charged with rape by force or fear or with having consensual sex with an person incapacitated due to intoxication or mental capacity), a motion for bill of particulars can be helpful in determining the specific factual allegations that form the basis for the charge.

Forcing the prosecutor to provide a more precise factual allegation is helpful to preparing a defense. It eliminates the need to guess the factual scenario that could be presented by the prosecutor at trial.

I often use this type of motion to clarify the date on which a crime is alleged to have occurred. Prosecutors do not have to allege the exact date and time of the crime in the charging document. Instead, they can allege that a crime took place in between a significant block of time; so long as the alleged block of time falls within the statute of limitations. For example, the charging document can allege that the crime was committed between June 2004 and September 2004. This often happens in cases with alleged child victims and cases that involve a delay in reporting the crime.

The bill of particulars forces the prosecution to be more specific about the date and time of the crime charged (e.g., the week of July 7, 2004, in the afternoon) because the defendant may have an alibi or other defenses for many of the days in between the broader time period.

An extra benefit of a bill of particulars is that it locks the prosecutor into a factual premise that can be changed only upon a showing of good cause to the court—and definitely cannot be changed once trial begins, as it would cause an unfair surprise to the defense.

A sample Motion for Bill of Particulars is included as Exhibit S on the enclosed CD-ROM. ➥

MOTION TO CHANGE VENUE

This motion contends that the defendant cannot receive a fair trial in the jurisdiction in which the case is charged and requests that the case be transferred to another jurisdiction. Such motions may be granted in cases that have gained a lot of local publicity or that are related in some way to a judge or staff in the jurisdiction (for example, I have seen a change of venue granted when a district court judge's son was the crime victim).

A sample Motion to Change Venue is included as Exhibit T on the enclosed CD-ROM. ➥

MOTION TO DISQUALIFY THE JUDGE

This motion asserts that the judge has a conflict in hearing the case either because of a personal attachment or because of some predisposition toward the defense or the prosecutor. You must allege that the judge cannot be fair and impartial due to the conflict.

Often, the judge you assert a conflict with hears this motion and is the judge of her own conflict. Motions asking a judge to disqualify herself because she has sent the defendant to prison in the past or denied various motions usually fail unless the judge perceives that she has such a personal grudge against the defendant that she cannot be fair and impartial—and it is rare to have a judge admit openly that she cannot be fair and impartial in a particular matter. Her decision will be overturned on appeal only if she is found to have abused her discretion.

Make certain you have a legitimate reason to file this motion. You will lose your credibility with the court if you file these often and without asserting a compelling conflict of interest.

A sample Motion to Recuse Judge is included as Exhibit U on the enclosed CD-ROM. ➥

ALIBI NOTICE

An alibi argues that the defendant could not have committed the crime because he was in another place at the time the crime was committed. Because it is an affirmative defense, the defendant often has the burden to prove the alibi.

If the alibi defense is presented, most jurisdictions have a statutory deadline by which you must file a notice of alibi claiming that the defendant was at another place and listing all witnesses, locations, and addresses involved (if available). Ordinarily, you must provide any witness's last known address so that the prosecutor is given the opportunity to contact or investigate the witness. This differs from usual discovery rules, because ordinarily the defendant does not have to provide the names and addresses (or endorse) any of his non-expert witnesses during the discovery process because the prosecution has the burden of proof.

If the alibi notice is not timely given, the court may be entitled to preclude witness testimony on the alibi (but the court cannot preclude the defendant from testifying regarding his alibi because he has a constitutional right to testify).

A sample Alibi Notice is included as Exhibit V on the enclosed CD-ROM. ➥

INSANITY/MENTAL DISEASE OR DEFECT NOTICE

In an insanity defense, the defendant admits to committing the crime, but claims that she lacked the requisite mental capacity to appreciate the consequences of her own actions or to be in control of her faculties; that is, she lacked the ability to intend the consequences of her actions.

Ordinarily, you must give notice to the prosecutor of your intent to present this defense. Some jurisdictions require you to list in the notice any psychological expert that may be called to testify at trial as to this defense. Often, there is a statutory time limit in which to file this notice after the preliminary hearing or the arraignment.

A sample Notice of Insanity Defense is included as Exhibit W on the enclosed CD-ROM. ➥

PRETRIAL CONFERENCE ORDER

The pretrial conference order governs the format of the trial. Often, the purpose behind the pretrial conference order is to encourage the parties to take a look at their case: to agree, as much as possible, on the admission of evidence and to advise the court about contested facts and issues, the length of the case, and any novel issues that the case may involve. Ideally this will assure a quicker, smoother trial.

The pretrial conference order is ordinarily filed one to three months before trial and may outline the issues/orders addressed by the parties and the court during the pretrial conference. It will summarize the charges and the facts relied upon in support of them, and may include lists or descriptions of the following:

- ► All counsel that will appear at trial
- ► All expert witnesses that the parties may call, including their area of expertise and their addresses
- ► All exhibits that may be used at trial, including charts, graphs, models, schematic diagrams, and similar objects that may be utilized in opening statements and closing arguments, whether or not they will be offered as evidence
- ► Depositions or sworn testimony that will be read to the jury
- ► All pending or outstanding issues that require a ruling by the court
- ► Any affirmative defenses

The pretrial conference order will also include a list of stipulations, that is, agreements between the parties. For instance, the parties may agree to the admission of certain exhibits or statements without requiring the party who introduces the exhibit to lay a proper evidentiary foundation. This may save time for both parties.

Usually, both parties will file a proposed pretrial conference order and then join them into the final order.

A pretrial conference order can be beneficial to the defense for several reasons:

- ► It may detail the prosecutor's trial strategy.
- ► It may reveal certain issues that should be addressed with a motion in limine (discussed below).
- ► The prosecutor is often locked into the contentions, witnesses, and exhibits listed in the pretrial conference order and will be forbidden from changing them without the court's permission.

The drawbacks are

- ► They sometimes force the defense to disclose key elements of its strategy.
- ► The court may limit the introduction of issues that were not listed in the pretrial conference order.

A sample Pretrial Conference Order is included as Exhibit X on the enclosed CD-ROM. ➥

MOTION TO DISMISS

A motion to dismiss requests that the court dismiss the case. Some common grounds for such motions include lack of jurisdiction, lack of a speedy trial, and lack of sufficient evidence to proceed.

Lack of Jurisdiction

A motion to dismiss because the court lacks jurisdiction to hear the matter may be filed because

▶   The statute of limitations has run—this is a statutorily prescribed period of time within which a crime must be charged by the prosecution. The court loses jurisdiction to hear a criminal matter if it is filed after the statute of limitations has run.

▶   The state has failed to establish that the crime occurred within the court's jurisdiction—that is, within the city or county in which the court presides.

▶   The case is barred by double jeopardy, either because the defendant has already pled to or been tried for the same crime or because a material fact was at issue in a previous prosecution for another crime and the case was resolved by trial.

Lack of Speedy Trial

The defendant has a right to be brought to trial within a statutorily set period of time after a plea of "Not Guilty" is entered or the charges are filed. This period begins to run after the First Appearance for a misdemeanor and after the arraignment for a felony unless otherwise specified by statute. The period can be shorter for those defendants who are in custody and may be tolled, or extended, if the defendant is in custody for another charge or another matter.

Some jurisdictions have a speedy preliminary hearing rule. The defendant must be brought to a preliminary hearing within a statutorily set period of time or else he will be released from custody or the charges dismissed.

Lack of Sufficient Evidence to Proceed

A motion to dismiss for lack of sufficient evidence combines the facts presented by the prosecutor at the preliminary hearing or grand jury with a more in-depth analysis of the law and requests that the court dismiss the matter for lack of evidence or lack of probable cause. The motion may revisit the evidence presented at the preliminary hearing or grand jury, and it may include uncontroverted evidence that will inevitably be admitted at trial. This motion usually must be filed within a statutorily prescribed period of time after a preliminary hearing or grand jury indictment in which the defendant is bound over for trial. Ordinarily, it must be filed in order to preserve on objection to a court ruling raised during the preliminary hearing or to preserve an objection to a court ruling regarding the sufficiency of the grand jury's indictment.

I generally do not find these motions beneficial. Because they require criticizing the prosecutor's evidence and arguing why it is insufficient, these motions tend to give away the defense theory of the case to the prosecution before trial. If you lose the motion—which is likely, as the court views the evidence in a light most favorable to the prosecution—the prosecutor now has an opportunity to correct any deficiencies in her case before trial.

A sample Motion to Dismiss is included as Exhibit Y on the enclosed CD-ROM. ➥

MOTION TO SUPPRESS EVIDENCE

These motions request that the court prevent certain evidence from being introduced against the defendant at trial because it was obtained through illegal means, in violation of the defendant's Fourth, Fifth, or Sixth Amendment rights.

If the defense succeeds in having all of the pertinent evidence suppressed (e.g., the drugs in a possession case), then the court may dismiss the case on its own motion, upon a defense motion to dismiss, or upon a prosecution motion to dismiss.

Motions to suppress evidence are often based upon issues involving (1) illegally obtained evidence or (2) illegally obtained confessions and all evidence obtained from illegally obtained confessions.

Illegally Obtained Evidence

▶ *Evidence was obtained without a warrant, probable cause, or reasonable suspicion.* Generally, officers of the law cannot search a person, place, or motor vehicle without one of these grounds. The premise of this motion is that evidence should be suppressed because it was obtained in violation of the defendant's rights against unreasonable search and seizure. In other words, the police or governmental agent violated the defendant's Fourth Amendment rights.

▶ *Evidence was obtained with an invalid warrant.* If evidence was seized pursuant to a warrant, it may be suppressed if the defense can establish that the warrant was flawed because

  ▼ The application contains material falsities or misstatements of the truth.

▼ The warrant application fails to state sufficient grounds to constitute probable cause.

▼ Information contained in the application for warrant is from an untrustworthy confidential informant.

▼ The application was not supported by oath or affirmation.

▼ The application or the warrant fails to particularly describe the place to be searched or evidence to be seized.

▼ The warrant was not signed or issued by a person with the proper authority to issue a warrant.

► *Evidence was obtained by exceeding the authority of the warrant.* Evidence obtained pursuant to an otherwise lawful warrant may also be suppressed if the officers executing the warrant exceeded the bounds set out in the warrant. (e.g., they search a trailer in the backyard though it was not described in the warrant).

► *Evidence was obtained as a result of an illegal arrest.* A law enforcement officer must have an arrest warrant or sufficient statutorily authorized grounds to arrest an individual. Without a warrant or sufficient grounds for arrest, all evidence seized can be suppressed.

Illegally Obtained Confession

► *Statement was obtained in violation of* Miranda. Generally, a confession may be suppressed if it was obtained without notifying the defendant of his right to remain silent and his right to have an attorney present. These are the *Miranda* rights. *Miranda* applies only to situations in which the totality of the circumstances establishes that the defendant was "in custody" while making the statements requested to be suppressed, and actually being interrogated or specifically questioned by law enforcement officers while making those statements.

Voluntary admissions before being advised of *Miranda* rights are not suppressable. For example, if defendant is sitting in a police car, and before she is questioned by a police officer, she states, "Why am I under arrest? All I did is hide a gun for some guy," her statement is a voluntary statement because it was not the result of questioning by police officers.

► *Statement was not obtained after a free and voluntary waiver of* Miranda *rights.* Even if *Miranda* is administered, the *Miranda* waiver or any statement made following such waiver must be made freely and voluntarily by the defendant. The following are some general grounds that constitute a challenge to the free and voluntary nature of the confession:

▼ The defendant was beaten or abused during the interrogation.

▼ Law enforcement officers made inappropriate promises or threats during the interrogation that induced the statement.

▼ Should the client not speak English, the interpreter who assisted the officer during the interrogation was biased, ineffective, or uncertified.

▼ The defendant was mentally incompetent and could not understand the *Miranda* warning, its waiver, or the nature and the extent of the interrogation and therefore could not freely and voluntarily give a statement.

▼ The defendant was intoxicated to the point that he could not understand the *Miranda* warning, its waiver, or the nature and the extent of the interrogation and therefore could not freely and voluntarily give a statement.

A sample Motion to Suppress is included as Exhibit Z on the enclosed CD-ROM. ➥

MOTION FOR SEPARATE JURY TRIAL

This motion is used (1) to request that the court separate the trials of codefendants; (2) to request that unrelated charges be tried separately, or (3) to request separate trials for the offense charged and an element that enhances the severity level of the offense charged.

Separate Trials for Codefendants

Generally, courts will separate the trials of codefendants when one defendant has made a statement incriminating himself and the other defendant. That is because statements of coconspirators cannot be used against a criminal defendant in his trial (unless the statements are made in furtherance of and in the course of a criminal conspiracy). This is known as the *Bruton* rule.[1]

Separate Trials for Unrelated Charges

Sometimes, the prosecutor will charge in the same charging document unrelated crimes that occurred on different occasions. The motion for separate trials claims that the defendant will be substantially prejudiced in his right to a fair trial if the separate charges are tried together. The concern is that the jury will unfairly consider the evidence for one charge to convict the defendant of the other charge.

---

[1] *See Bruton v. United States,* 391 U.S. 123 (1968) (defendant's right to confrontation was violated when there was admitted into evidence the "powerfully incriminating extrajudicial statements of codefendant, who stands accused side-by-side with the defendant").

For example, a single trial involving the charge of possession of methamphetamine on January 11, 2004, and the charge of sale of methamphetamine on December 24, 2005, may substantially prejudice the defendant's right to a fair trial. If the evidence for the possession case is strong, but the evidence for the sale case is very weak, the jury may unfairly convict the defendant for the sale charge. In other words, the jury may unfairly presume that because he is guilty of the first crime, he must be guilty of the second crime.

Separate Trials for the Offense Charged and an Enhancing Element

Sometimes, an element of a crime involves defendant having been convicted of a previous crime. For example:

▶ DUI, second offense, requires the prosecution to prove that the defendant has been convicted of DUI once before as an element of the crime.

▶ Possession of a weapon by a previous offender requires the prosecution to prove that the defendant has been convicted of a previous offense, which statutorily prohibits the defendant from possessing a weapon, as an element of the crime.

In these cases, if the motion for separate trials is granted, the issue of the actual crime is handled in one trial and the issue of the previous conviction is handled after, in a second trial, only if the jury convicts in the first trial. This is beneficial to the defense because you do not want the jury to merely convict the defendant based upon his past criminal history. Lots of people believe that if the defendant has a criminal conviction in his past, then it is more likely true than not that he is guilty in the present case, regardless of the evidence. They tend to believe he has a propensity to commit crimes. Although they are not supposed to do this, the chance of the prejudice is great. Therefore, if you can keep your client's criminal history out of the guilt phase, you should always do so.

A sample Motion for Separate Jury Trial is included as Exhibit AA on the enclosed CD-ROM. ➛

MOTION IN LIMINE

A motion in limine requests that the court order certain evidence inadmissible at trial because such admission would violate a specified rule of evidence, the evidence is irrelevant, or the prejudicial effect of the evidence upon the jury substantially outweighs its relevance or probative value. If the judge grants the motion, no one can address the excluded evidence during the trial.

Any potential evidence that you feel will prejudice the defendant's right to a fair trial can be the subject of a motion in limine. Examples of issues you may want to address on a motion in limine:

▶ The defendant was previously arrested for the same offense.

▶ Any evidence of defendant's gang affiliation.

▶ Lay witness giving expert testimony (the police report may have officers making comments that they have no expertise to make; e.g., the trajectory of a bullet, the cause of an accident, that injuries appear to be defensive wounds, etc.)

▶ The fact that the victim was on his way to volunteer at a soup kitchen.

My motion often includes the following prayer, as I want the prosecutor forbidden at all times from mentioning the evidence sought to be excluded:

> Defendant, John Doe, by and through his attorney of record, Jane Litigator, moves this Court for an Order in Limine to instruct all parties, their counsel, and their witnesses not to attempt to introduce into evidence, make any reference to in voir dire, in opening statement and closing argument, elicit by examination or cross-examination, or otherwise leave the jury with any impression to the following: . . .

A sample Motion in Limine is included as Exhibit BB on the enclosed CD-ROM. ➻

PROPOSED JURY INSTRUCTIONS

Before trial, judges often require the parties to submit proposed jury instructions. These are rules of law that either party desires to have the jury instructed upon at the closing of the evidence. Ideally, the jury takes the instructions upon the law, applies the facts presented during trial, and makes a determination as to whether the prosecutor has proved the charges beyond a reasonable doubt.

Most jurisdictions have "form" or "pattern" instructions from which to choose. These instructions are put together by a panel of purported experts in the field—often district court judges and appellate court judges. The instructions are usually taken directly from the wording of the underlying statutory and case law.

Sometimes a rule of law that you desire to be given to the jury may not be contained in the book of pattern instructions. If this occurs, draft a proposed instruction parroting the rule of law from the particular case that you have taken it from. Thereafter, cite to the appropriate case below the body of the proposed instruction in a footnote.

A sample Proposed Jury Instructions is included as Exhibit CC on the enclosed CD-ROM. ⊷

TRIAL BRIEF

A trial brief in a criminal case contains an argument as to why the court should apply a particular law to the facts of the case during the trial or why the court should instruct the jury on a certain issue. Often, they are filed before trial, along with the proposed instructions. Sometimes it may become necessary to file a trial brief during the middle of trial if a dispute arises as to the appropriate law to be applied by the court.

A judge may request that each party submit a trial brief at the closing of all evidence in a bench trial, setting out the reasons for the court to rule in its favor, citing to the facts and law that support each party's position.

A sample Trial Brief is included as Exhibit DD on the enclosed CD-ROM. ⊷

TIPS FOR FOR DRAFTING MOTIONS

1. *Copy the motion from someone else.* You do not have to reinvent the wheel. Start writing your motions by reviewing and copying the format from a similar motion filed by another attorney. You may even copy the language of the other motion that is relevant to your issue. Reviewing a similar motion drafted by another attorney may also help you realize that you have an additional novel issue that must be addressed.

    ▼ Research the case law cited in the motion to make certain that it actually stands for the issue you desire to use it for.

    ▼ Expound on the law if additional or more recent law has addressed the issue since the motion's writing.

    ▼ Mold the necessary language of the motion to fit with your facts.

    To find motions written by other attorneys:

    ▼ Ask your colleagues if they have written a similar motion or other criminal defense attorneys if they have addressed the issue with a motion.

    ▼ Go to the clerk of the trial court and check out several files involving cases of highly respected or prominent defense attorneys.

    ▼ Copy the whole file or merely the motion you need.

▼ Keep looking through files until you find what you want.

2. *Draft the motion according to the FIRAC method.* FIRAC stands for facts, issue, rule, analysis and conclusion. You were probably taught this format of legal writing in law school. It is a method to control your writing, enabling anyone who reads your writing to spot the issues immediately and to understand your point without thoroughly reading your brief. Easy issue-spotting can be important because there are a few judges out there that will not always read your motion thoroughly.

FIRAC contemplates the following order and content:

▼ *Facts.* The first section should contain the charges and the facts alleged by the prosecution to support the charges or the facts at issue in your motion. (You will find these in the police reports or the Affidavit of Probable Cause.)

▼ *Issue.* The next section should be a brief statement of the issue involved. Sometimes I include an issues section in the motion that outlines the issues to be resolved, much like an issues section contained in an appellate brief. For example:

ISSUES INVOLVED IN THIS MOTION TO SUPPRESS

I. WHETHER ALL STATEMENTS GIVEN TO THE ARRESTING OFFICERS BY DEFENDANT SHOULD BE SUPPRESSED AS VIOLATIVE OF THE FIFTH AMENDMENT AS DEFENDANT WAS NEVER GIVEN *MIRANDA* RIGHTS.

A. The Arresting Officer failed to provide defendant with *Miranda* warnings.

B. The law provides that defendant's statements given pursuant to a custodial interrogation shall be suppressed if *Miranda* warnings were not given.

C. The defendant was "in custody" at the time his statement was given to the arresting officer.

D. The defendant's statement was provided in response to an interrogation.

▼ *Rule.* This section states the rule of law that applies. Section I.B. above states the rule of law applicable in this issue.

▼ *Analysis.* This section applies the relevant facts at issue, as set out in the Facts Section, to the law, as set out in the Rule Section, and then purports to explain to the court why the law requires that defendant's motion be granted.

▼ *Conclusion.* This is a conclusory paragraph requesting the court to rule in favor of the defendant's position. Often, I am not very wordy in my conclusion and, as I would have already stated the conclusion I would like the court to arrive at in my analysis section, my conclusion is usually quite brief. For example:

WHEREFORE, for the reasons stated herein, the defendant respectfully requests this court to grant this motion and suppress the evidence at issue and for any other relief as the court finds just and equitable.

3. *Avoid making overconfident assertions or conclusions in your writing.* Judges dislike it when attorneys include overconfident statements such as, "It is clear that . . ." or "This court would be violating the law if it did not find. . . ." This rhetoric can be taken by the court for a misrepresentation or misstatement of the law by defense counsel.

4. *Create a motion/brief bank.* Keep a copy of every motion you file and a copy of any motion you see that is well written and may someday be germane to an issue that you are litigating. Eventually you will find that you have an entire library of motions. You may want to organize your motion/brief bank by the name of the motion.

CHAPTER 6

Arguing in Court

SPEAKING IN OPEN COURT

Everyone has the nervous jitters when first speaking in open court. Therefore, do not worry if you are initially frightened of speaking in open court. When I first began to practice law, I had years of public speaking practice under my belt: plays, forensics, debate (high school and college), student government, student counsel, girls state, student congress, moot court, and trial advocacy. I had spent most of my high school, college, and law school time preparing to be a trial lawyer. And yet, I was terrified when I stood up to make my first argument in open court. I still get nervous in certain situations.

I have found that the more arguments you make in front of the court, the more comfortable you will feel. The Rosetta Stone to overcoming fear of oral arguments is to be well prepared. In addition, follow these basic rules in making your arguments in open court.

TIPS FOR MAKING ORAL ARGUMENTS IN OPEN COURT

1. *Be prepared.* Know the authority for and against your position. (Have two copies of the important authority in favor of your position; one for the judge and one for the prosecutor.)

    ▼ Know the facts of your case and your argument well enough to distinguish authority adverse to your position.

    ▼ Anticipate the arguments that the prosecutor will make and tailor your argument to address any concerns that may arise from the prosecutor's contentions.

2. *Practice, practice, practice.* Rehearsing arguments in front of mirrors, on the drive to work, or in the shower will pay off when you're before the judge.

3. *Show dignity and respect in the courtroom.*

    ▼ Stand when addressing the court. If your local rule allows attorneys to be seated when addressing the court, stand until the court tells you it is okay to remain seated. However, you're better off standing, if possible: Sitting compresses the diaphragm, thus affecting your ability to project and inflect your voice, which inhibits the effectiveness of your argument.

    ▼ Use the courtroom furniture appropriately. Stand at the lectern provided when addressing the court. If you wish to stand at your table while addressing the court, ask permission. (Sometimes, you will have numerous papers and exhibits you will be referring to during a court argument, and it may be easier to address the court from your table where you have easy access to these materials.)

    ▼ Do not lean on the lectern. It is disrespectful to the judge and it looks sloppy.

    ▼ Never interrupt the court or the prosecutor.

4. *Consider your audience.* Judges are often assigned to hearings at the last moment and may know nothing about the case. Keeping your argument succinct and simple will keep you in the court's good graces.

    ▼ Ask the judge if she would like a brief recitation of the facts at issue before beginning your argument.

    ▼ Argue from an assumption that the court has not thoroughly read your brief. Tell the judge, in outline form, exactly how many issues you would like him to resolve and exactly what the issues involve. Then address each issue separately, highlighting the key points in your brief that address the issue. For example:

        Your Honor, defendant is charged with the crime of rape. There are two things I request from the court today.

        First, I would like Your Honor to suppress all statements made by the defendant after his arrest.

        Second, I would like you to find the defendant's arrest to be unlawful and thereafter suppress all evidence seized subsequent to this unlawful arrest.

        Would Your Honor like a brief recitation of the facts at issue? . . .

        In regard to the first suppression issue, the statement should be suppressed because defendant was never given a *Miranda* warning. . . .

In regard to the second suppression issue, any evidence seized as a result of the arrest should be suppressed because the defendant's arrest was unlawful. This is the case because the arresting officers lacked probable cause to arrest and failed to properly obtain a search warrant . . .

▼   Do not read your brief or pleading verbatim. The judge can read your brief himself, so do not read it to him when making your argument.

5. *Ask permission of the court before responding to or rebutting the prosecutor's argument.*

CHAPTER 7

Plea Agreement

Often, the defendant desires his attorney to approach the prosecutor for a plea offer. As described in Chapter 2, an attorney cannot approach the prosecutor and initiate plea negotiations without permission from the client.

EFFECTIVELY NEGOTIATING A PLEA

Negotiating a plea is much like playing poker: "You've gotta know when to hold 'em; know when to fold 'em; know when to walk away, and know when to run." You never show your hand until it is time to lay down your cards.

Before you decide to negotiate a plea, determine the winnability of the case. Ask yourself, "Is this a possible winner, a dead-bang loser, or one with 50-50 odds given the right jury panel?" Some factors to consider in making this determination are

- The defendant's appeal to a jury.
- Facts revealed through your own investigation of the prosecutor's facts. (You may hire an investigator to investigate the facts that appear in the discovery.)
- The prosecutor's reputation. Ask other criminal defense attorneys if the prosecutor tries close cases, refuses to make reasonable deals, or has legendary courtroom skills.
- The judge's reputation and ruling history.
- Your comfort level with your trial skills.
- Your confidence in the case after review of the discovery, facts, and preliminary hearing and grand jury testimony. Assessing a case's potential trial outcome becomes easier with trial experience, but even experienced attorneys should seek out the opinions of other experienced criminal defense attorneys. I discuss all of my cases and their potential trial outcomes with my law partner, Susan Martin.

If you decide to pursue a plea, ask your client what sort of offer she will settle for: a full dismissal; a misdemeanor with probation or a certain length of sentence; a lesser felony than what is charged (with a certain length of sentence or probation); serving time for one of the crimes charged with a dismissal of other counts; plead as charged with a reduced sentence or a recommendation of probation from the prosecutor; and so on. Then tell the prosecutor your client is interested in plea negotiations. Plea deals can be negotiated over the phone, by letter or e-mail, on the courthouse steps, in the prosecutor's office, or over the phone, depending on the case, the prosecutor's schedule, and the defense attorney's schedule.

TIPS FOR PLEA NEGOTIATIONS

1. *Avoid bidding against yourself.* A prosecutor never extends your dream offer at the beginning but will ask you to tell her what you want. This is the tricky part, and this is why I warn not to bid against yourself. If the client is willing to serve a year sentence but would like you to try first to get him probation, avoid beginning negotiations by telling the prosecutor that the client is willing to serve time. In a prosecutor's mind, if a client is willing to serve a year, then he is willing to serve longer so long as it is not the highest amount of time prescribed by statute for the offense. Revealing that fact at the beginning constitutes bidding against yourself. Whenever the prosecutor asks me what I want, I tell her that I do not want to bid against myself. I thereafter state, "No, you have to tell me what your best offer is going to be."

2. *Understand that the prosecutor's first offer is often not her best offer.* Sometimes the best offers are not made until the eve of trial.

3. *Don't tell the prosecutor that you dislike your client or believe he is guilty.* Sometimes revealing these facts closes the door to meaningful negotiations.

4. *Avoid pestering the prosecutor.* I believe repeated requests for a plea offer on the same case send a message to the prosecutor that you are desperate and unwilling to try the case. Some attorneys disagree with me on this point; they feel that consistent and persistent requests wear prosecutors down and push them to compromise. I have seen defense attorneys who succeed in this tactic, but I am told by prosecutors that these attorneys are not respected and ordinarily get worse deals than other attorneys.

5. *Advise the prosecutor of your client's good character or his disabilities.* I may tell the prosecutor anything true about the defendant that could win favor or sympathy: that my client has no criminal history, was honorably discharged from the Navy, is a single parent supporting four children, has

a college degree, checked himself into substance abuse or anger management treatment as a result of the arrest, is schizophrenic, or has stage 2
lymphoma.

6. *Never give away your entire defense or theory of the case.* You do not want
the negotiations to fall through and then be left with the prosecutor
knowing your entire defense strategy. There is no bright line as to how
much information you should reveal, but if you have to draw on the facts
of the case during negotiations, first rely on the undisputed facts.

For further guidance, see Chapter 4, Pretrial Communication with the Prosecutor and the Court.

DECIDING WHETHER TO ADVISE THE CLIENT TO ACCEPT A PLEA AGREEMENT

There is really no bright line in deciding whether to advise your client to accept
a plea agreement. My general rule is that if my client will receive the same sentence with a plea agreement that she would receive if she loses at trial, I advise
the client to reject the plea offer and to take her chances with trial. This is
because the client will have nothing to lose by taking the case to trial.

Anything can happen at a jury trial. Many times, when there was nothing
to lose by trying the case, I have received an acquittal or a conviction of a
lesser offense. Even in those instances when the client lost and was sentenced
to what she was offered in the plea agreement, I consider it a win: The client
made the prosecutor earn the conviction and sentence. And I learn something
new about the prosecutor, the judge, and myself every time I try a case.

REVIEWING AND COMMUNICATING THE PLEA OFFER WITH THE CLIENT

Every offer made by the prosecution must be communicated to the defendant. You will often find yourself going back and forth between the client and
the prosecutor before an offer is finally accepted. Sometimes the defendant
will get exactly what he wants and sometimes he will have to settle for something different.

There are two basic rules in discussing a plea offer with the defendant:

▶ *Never force, pressure, or threaten the defendant to accept a plea offer.* A
defendant must freely and voluntarily enter into a plea agreement. Forcing or pressuring a defendant to accept an offer is unethical and grounds

for the court to set aside the plea and have you removed from the case. This type of pressure is sometimes called "strong-arming." Some examples of inappropriate strong-arming are

▼ *Lying to the client about certain consequences should he not accept the plea.* For example, an attorney states, "Listen, if you do not accept this offer, you are guaranteed to go to prison for at least 20 years," when he knows the maximum potential sentence is eight years.

A Colorado public defender allegedly once told his client that he would not have the slightest idea of how to begin to defend her against the felony charges of forgery and evading and eluding a law enforcement office after a hit and run accident. I know that this public defender had been practicing for at least ten years and had litigated far more difficult cases. His statement was offensive, unethical, and a clear instance of strong-arming.

▼ *Assuring the client that the judge will follow the plea agreement.* The judge is never a party to the plea agreement and is therefore not bound to follow it. The judge can sentence the defendant to any legal sentence she desires, ignoring the plea agreement entirely. Make this point very clear to the defendant.

Clients will likely ask your opinion regarding the chance that the judge will follow the agreement. I have answered, "I cannot promise or assure you that the judge will follow the agreement. However, I have seen this judge sentence many defendants in similar situations and I have never seen her refuse to follow agreements similar to this."

▼ *Threatening the client.* It is not acceptable to make any threat to the client should she refuse to accept the plea offer. I have heard tales of attorneys threatening to purposely lose the trial or reveal privileged information. That is morally wrong and I hope those attorneys get disbarred.

► *Require the defendant to sign an acknowledgement of the plea and waiver of certain rights.* Have the defendant sign something that indicates that

▼ He understands the plea offer.

▼ He understands the rights he is giving up in entering into the plea (the right to a trial, to appeal any trial errors, and to remain silent).

▼ He has not been coerced by anyone to enter into the plea: he is knowingly and voluntarily entering into the plea, and there have been no threats or promises made to him forcing him to accept the offer.

▼ He understands that the judge is not a party to the plea, and that the judge can sentence the defendant to any legal sentence he desires, ignoring the plea agreement entirely.

A sample Plea Agreement is included as Exhibit EE on the enclosed CD-ROM. ••

PUTTING THE CLIENT'S PLEA ON THE RECORD

A judge must accept the client's plea pursuant to the plea agreement in open court. (This can be waived if the defendant pleads to a traffic offense or certain low-level crimes, depending on the jurisdiction.) This is often called a plea or disposition hearing.

Sometimes, a formal plea decree or agreement is signed, acknowledged on the record, and filed in the court file. Often, the judge will make a complete record of the defendant's acknowledgement of his waiver of certain trial rights and entry of plea. Sometimes, the entire agreement is read into the record by the judge or prosecutor.

Judges like to be certain that the plea is entered into knowingly and voluntarily. Judges usually advise the defendant that the sentencing judge is not bound by the agreement and can sentence the defendant to whatever legal sentence the judge deems appropriate.

Frequently, a factual basis is required to accept the plea. This is a recitation of the facts by the defendant or the prosecutor that supports the conviction for the crime to which the defendant is pleading guilty or no contest. A factual basis is often required by statute as legislators do not want innocent defendants entering guilty pleas.

A sample Transcript of Plea and Sentencing Hearing is included as Exhibit FF on the enclosed CD-ROM. ••

WITHDRAWING THE CLIENT'S PLEA AFTER IT HAS BEEN ACCEPTED BY THE COURT

Too often, defendants decide to withdraw the plea entered pursuant to the plea agreement. Ordinarily, in order to withdraw the plea the defendant must prove to the court that the plea was not knowingly and voluntarily entered into.

This may create a conflict for the attorney who negotiated the plea because proving such often requires proof that the attorney failed in reviewing and communicating the plea offer to the defendant. Where this occurs, the attorney must withdraw and a new attorney must be retained or appointed to argue that the plea was invalid. This is because the original attorney who negotiated and argued the plea, may be required to testify at the proceeding to determine whether the defendant should be allowed to withdraw his plea.

Some common grounds that support a motion to withdraw a plea on the basis that it was not knowingly and voluntarily entered into are

► *The defendant was incompetent when he entered into the agreement.* Competency to enter into a plea agreement is defined as either (1) the same competency needed to enter into a binding contract or (2) competency to stand trial. In withdrawing a plea, the defendant may be required to establish one or all of the following:

   ▼ He was not competent to understand the plea offer.

   ▼ He did not understand the rights he was waiving.

   ▼ He did not understand the potential consequences of entering into a plea according to the plea agreement.

   ▼ Due to one or all of these reasons, he did not freely, knowingly, and voluntarily enter into the plea agreement.

► *The defendant was under the influence of drugs or alcohol.* The defendant may be able to withdraw his plea if he can establish that he was under the influence of drugs or alcohol to the point that

   ▼ He could not understand the plea offer.

   ▼ He could not understand the rights he was waiving.

   ▼ He could not understand the potential consequences of entering into a plea according to the plea agreement.

   ▼ Due to one or all of these reasons, he did not freely, knowingly, and voluntarily enter into the plea agreement.

There can be negative consequences for the defendant if he claims he was under the influence at the time of the plea.

   ▼ He may subject himself to violating the condition of his bond if it was conditioned upon his not using drugs or alcohol while on bond.

   ▼ If he claims he was under the influence of illegal drugs, he may subject himself to a new crime for violating the conditions of his bond, because all bonds require that the defendant refrain from committing any new crimes.

Once I had a client who was in jail at the time of the plea review and the plea hearing. At his motion to withdraw plea he claimed that he was under the influence of drugs both at the time I reviewed the plea agreement with him and when he entered the plea. The judge easily and generously granted the client's request and thereafter requested the prosecutor to file felony charges for trafficking contraband in a jail facility for having possessed and used drugs while in jail. In the end, the client received an additional felony and a sentence greater than that contemplated by the plea agreement. Given my client's negative outcome under these circumstances, you may want to advise your client of similar possibilities should he find himself in similar circumstances and requests you to file a motion to withdraw his plea.

▶ *The attorney failed to completely advise the defendant of the conditions of the entire plea agreement.* If the attorney fails to review all of the conditions of the plea agreement, then the defendant may be able to withdraw his plea. The defendant must establish that the failure to properly advise kept him from freely and voluntarily enter into the plea agreement.

CHAPTER 8

Preparing for Trial

A good defense attorney prepares for trial throughout the entire client relationship, regardless of whether the client has requested that the attorney settle the matter. This is because plea negotiations fall through or the desired plea offer is not usually extended until the eve or morning of trial. However, more than 95% of all cases are pled out without going to trial.

The following points will assist you in preparing for trial.

INVESTIGATE THE FACTS OF THE CASE

Know Your Discovery

Read all discovery documents provided through the discovery process. This includes all police reports, medical records, and expert reports provided by the prosecution. If you do not know how to read various records and reports, you must learn how.

TIPS FOR REVIEWING MEDICAL RECORDS

Medical records are not always simple to review. If you have no medical experience, you may need to consult medical dictionaries, anatomical charts, and anything that can help you decipher the notations in the record.

1. *Start by reading the typewritten reports.* They may help you decipher certain handwritten notes, observations, or abbreviations.

2. *Compile a medical-reference library.*

   ▼ A medical dictionary or encyclopedia, for looking up the various diagnoses, symptoms, drugs, and body parts, can be purchased at most large bookstore chains or in college bookstores. I have found *The Mosby Medical Encyclopedia,* Revised Edition (Plume Publishing, 1992) to be quite helpful.

▼ A book of color anatomical charts will assist you in reading the reports. These can be purchased at most large bookstore chains or college bookstores as well. I have found *The World's Best Anatomical Charts,* Second Edition (Skolkie, IL: Anatomical Chart Co., 1995) to be quite helpful.

▼ Consult a legal reference book on how to analyze medical records if you are having some difficulties in deciphering the medical reports. I have found *Analyzing Medical Records for the Kansas Paralegal* (Institute for Paralegal Education NBI, 1999) to be very helpful. (I got it at a paralegal continuing education course I attended in Overland Park, Kansas.)

▼ The annual *Physicians Desk Reference* (*PDR*) lists nearly every drug ever made with its side effects, the symptoms it is prescribed for, and its generic name. A *PDR* can be purchased at most large bookstore chains or at college bookstores on university campuses that have nursing or medical degree programs.

3. *Consult experts.* Ask your family physician to explain unfamiliar terms and phrases, or to recommend a specialist you might consult with. Or ask your fellow attorneys or the staff at a nearby medical school for referrals.

4. *Ask the author.* Contact the actual physician or nurse who authored the record and ask her to help you decipher what is in the medical records. Consider it a good thing if she refuses to speak with you because that reveals a bias in favor of the prosecution, which you may bring up on cross-examination.

A sample Medical Report is attached as Exhibit GG. ➻

TIPS FOR REVIEWING EXPERT REPORTS

Expert reports include ballistics examination reports, tool mark examination reports, autopsy reports, fingerprint comparison reports, DNA comparison reports, accident reconstruction reports, psychological evaluation reports, and toxicology reports.

1. *Familiarize yourself with the subject of the report.*

▼ An Internet search will likely provide you with enough articles on a particular subject to help you to become reasonably informed.

▼ Your local law school library should contain numerous books on every expert subject that may be addressed in a criminal case. It will also have periodicals that specialize in the subject or that contain articles that address the subject.

▼ The closest university library will probably have books on numerous criminal investigation subjects.

2. *Ask another expert* to help you interpret the expert's findings in the report.

3. *Contact the author of the report.* Ask if she has time to explain certain matters contained in the report. As with medical reports, consider it a good thing if the expert refuses to speak with you. It reveals the supposedly neutral and impartial expert's bias in favor of the prosecution, which you may bring that issue up on cross-examination.

4. *Contact the reporting expert's supervisor.* See if that person may be of some assistance in interpreting the report.

A sample Expert Report is included as Exhibit HH on the enclosed CD-ROM.

Visit the Scene of the Crime

You will never fully understand the prosecutor's allegations and your client's contentions if you do not visit the scene of the crime. Additionally, visiting the crime scene often turns up valuable evidence that is not mentioned in the police reports. Visit the scene as many times as you need to in order to familiarize yourself with the scene and to help you understand or explain certain concepts.

TIPS FOR VISITING THE SCENE OF THE CRIME

1. *Familiarize yourself with the entire area.* For example, see if the house is in a bad neighborhood. A high-crime neighborhood may assist your theory that someone else could have committed the crime.

2. *Take notes.*

3. *Draw a diagram.* Even if it is crude, it will help you remember the location of key things for trial.

4. *Shoot photos.* (A picture of an alleged victim's trashy, rundown trailer identified as the alleged scene of the crime creates a vivid image for the jury as to the type of person the victom may be.)

5. *Take measurements if distance is relevant to your strategy of the case.*

6. *If possible, reenact movements alleged to have occurred during the crime.* Visiting the crime scene sometimes shows that certain events relayed by witnesses are physically impossible. I once had a murder case in which it was alleged that the defendant walked from one apartment building to another in a certain amount of time. I sent an investigator out to measure the distance and determine the length of time required to walk that distance. Sure enough, he found that the prosecution's claims were impossible.

Hire a Private Investigator

Delegating legwork to an investigator will not only save your time, it will also put the investigator, and not you, on the witness stand to testify to any facts discovered. Among the tasks for which you might use an investigator:

▶ Interview witnesses and record their statements

▶ Testify at trial about a witness's interview statements that are inconsistent with the witness's trial testimony, and establish foundation to admit the interview statement into evidence

▶ Photograph the crime scene and testify at trial to establish the foundation for the admission of the photographs

▶ Testify about her own observations of the scene or the evidence

▶ Track down witnesses who will testify favorably for the defense and obtain statements from them

▶ Serve subpoenas on any witnesses whose testimony may be helpful to the defense strategy

▶ Track down records or physical evidence that may be helpful to the defense strategy

Interview Key Witnesses

Have your investigator find key witnesses and take their statements. If you are a control freak like me and insist on conducting many interviews yourself, it is still important to involve an investigator to take notes during the interview and record the witness's statements.

▶ If the witness testifies differently at trial, your investigator can be called to testify about the inconsistent statements the witness made during your interview. This keeps you from becoming a witness, which is bad because it is unethical for the attorney to testify as a witness for his client. The court may forbid the introduction of the attorney's testimony or even order a mistrial.

▶ Recording the interview is helpful because even good, honest witnesses can testify differently from the statements that they made to you and your investigator during the interview. The witness can be impeached with the recording.

▶ The recording also protects the attorney or the investigator from any allegation made by the witness that the attorney or investigator was abusive during the interview.

The negative side to recording interviews is that the court may order you to produce a copy of the recording to the prosecution, or require you to play the whole interview tape to the jury if you decide to play one part of the tape to show the witness's contradiction. There may be just as many favorable statements for the prosecution on the tape as there are for the defense.

Examine All Physical Evidence

As with the crime scene, you will never fully understand the prosecutor's allegations and your client's contentions if you do not examine all of the physical evidence before trial. A physical examination often reveals discrepancies from crime scene pictures or photocopies taken of the same piece of evidence and provided to the defense in discovery. For example, the shoes found by the police and alleged to have trace evidence on them may not be the defendant's size.

Particularly when there are no pictures of the physical evidence, an examination may reveal that it differs from its description in the investigating officers' report. I was once involved in a case where the codefendant was alleged to have swung a bat at the victims. From the police report, one would assume that the weapon was a large wooden baseball bat. However, my examination of the physical evidence revealed that this bat was an 18-inch by 1.25-inch souvenir baseball bat. It was not as imposing as the officer made it sound in his report.

Issue Subpoenas

If you determine through your investigation of the facts of the case that a witness can give testimony that will be favorable to your theory of the case, have the witness subpoenaed to appear at trial.

► A subpoena is a command by the court, at the request of a party, to appear at a certain time and place to give testimony upon a certain matter.

► A subpoena duces tecum, or subpoena to produce, is a subpoena that further orders the witness to bring specified items along with him. You may issue these during the course of your investigation of the case in order to obtain documents that may be relevant to the defense, such as employment records, telephone records, medical records, school records, or banking transaction records.

Ordinarily, the attorney must sign the subpoena and file a copy of the same with the court. Some jurisdictions require that the clerk of the court sign the subpoena. Check your jurisdiction's subpoena service rule to determine who can serve subpoenas. Sometimes the individual serving the subpoena must be certified by the court to serve subpoenas.

A sample Subpoena Duces Tecum (also referred to as a Subpoena to Appear and Produce) is included as Exhibit II on the enclosed CD-ROM. ➝

REVIEW ALL RELEVANT LAWS AND RULES

► Review the statutes under which the defendant is charged, paying particular attention to the required elements of proof. Make a copy of the statutes for your file.

► Review the pattern jury instructions and make a copy for your file.

► Review the caselaw discussing the particular criminal statute in order to draft a jury instruction that may not appear in the pattern instruction book or to brief or argue a point of law to the court.

► Review the rules of evidence regarding admission of certain evidence or testimony and exclusion of certain evidence or testimony.

► Develop a plan involving the rules of evidence that you will rely on to introduce evidence and to try to exclude evidence.

DEVELOP YOUR TRIAL STRATEGY

Trial strategy is your plan to attack the prosecutor's case and establish the defense strategy to win the case. There are three basic steps to developing a trial strategy: develop a theory of your case; consider which facts support your theory ("good facts") and which support the prosecutor's theory ("bad facts"); and decide whether to call expert witnesses.

Develop a Theory of the Case

The theory of the case is the defendant's one-sentence statement to the jury explaining why he is not guilty. It is the defendant's version of events that contradicts the state's version of events and that will lead the jury to believe that the defendant is not guilty.

The following are a few examples of case theories:

► The defendant is not guilty because he was in another place at another time, therefore making it impossible for him to have committed the crime (the alibi defense—remember, this defense often requires a special notification to the prosecutor).

► The defendant is not guilty because someone else committed the crime.

▶ The defendant is not guilty because a crime never occurred. The victim fabricated the crime and the defendant's involvement.

▶ The defendant is not guilty because he was entrapped.

▶ The defendant did not commit the crime as charged. He committed a less severe crime.

▶ The defendant is not guilty because of insanity or mental disease or defect. (Remember, this defense often requires a special notification to the prosecutor.)

▶ The defendant is not guilty because he acted in self-defense.

Trial strategizing should begin with picking a theory of the case. It is possible to have more than one theory of the defense, but I do not advise it, as additional theories may contradict (although it is legally permissible to have contradictory theories—i.e., the defendant was not there, but if he was, he did not do it).

Spot Good Facts and Bad Facts

When I first read through discovery I like to highlight the apparent good and bad facts for my client. The good facts support the defendant's innocence, and the bad facts support the prosecutor's theory of guilt.

I often make a columned list of the good facts beside the bad facts, noting the location of the fact in the discovery. When necessary, I make notes to myself to follow up certain facts. The following is an example:

Theory of the Case: The defendant is not guilty because he acted in self-defense.

Good Facts	Bad Facts
1. The shooting took place on defendant's front porch (O'Connor's rep. p. 2 ¶ 2)	1. Defendant shot victim (O'Connor's rep. p. 2 ¶ 3)
2. Victim weighs 275 lbs (check arrest record for Def's weight) (autopsy rep. p. 4)	2. Victim was shot three times (autopsy rep. p. 5)
3. Victim was 6'2" (check arrest record for Def's height) (autopsy rep. p. 4)	3. One of shots had entrance wound through back (autopsy rep. p. 6)

When all discovery and investigation is finished, I will review and add to this list. At that point, I can begin adding omissions of certain facts to my good facts section. For instance, if my client denies committing the crime and if there is a possibility that fingerprints could connect my client to the crime, I will note as a good fact that no attempt was made to examine the scene or the physical evidence for fingerprints.

By the end, I always manage to have more good facts than bad facts. If you look hard enough and creatively enough, keeping the theory of the case in mind, you can find more good facts than bad.

A sample Good Facts Example is included as Exhibit JJ, and a sample Bad Facts Example is included as Exhibit KK on the enclosed CD-ROM. ➴

Decide Whether to Use Expert Witnesses

Expert witnesses testify about issues that are outside of the common knowledge and understanding of a jury. Criminal trial experts may include

▶ Accident Reconstructionist: determines nature and cause of an accident, e.g., car accident

▶ Arson Investigator: determines if a fire was arson and the source of the fire

▶ Ballistics Expert: examines weapons and projectiles (bullets) and determines whether a specific weapon propelled a specific projectile

▶ Blood Spatter Examiner: examines pattern of blood spray to determine directionality, etc.

▶ Chemist: analyzes the chemical makeup of substances, including drugs, to identify them

▶ Computer Information System Specialist: retrieves deleted data from a computer or testifies about the various workings, capabilities, and functions of a computer

▶ Crime Scene Examiner: specializes in collecting physical evidence at the crime scene

▶ Firearms Expert: specializes in the characteristics of firearms

▶ Geneticist or Microbiologist: conducts DNA testing

▶ Handwriting Examiner: examines handwriting samples and compares to writing from a known source

▶ Latent Print Examiner: conducts fingerprint comparison analysis

▶ Pathologist: conducts the autopsy, or postmortem examination, and determines cause of death

▶ Psychiatrist/Psychologist: conducts a psychological examination of the victim or the defendant

▶ Sexual Assault Nurse Examiner: an emergency-room nurse who specializes in conducting sexual assault exams

▶ Tool-Mark Examiner: examines instruments for striations or other markings that will tie the instrument to a scene; may include burglary tools, shoe markings

▶ Toxicologist: specializes in the effects, diagnosis, treatments, and antidotes of drugs and poisons; conducts toxicology blood screenings

▶ Treating Physician: examines and treats the injuries of the victim

Other experts may be required depending on your case. Any person who has knowledge outside of the common knowledge and understanding of the jury can be an expert witness.

Often, auto mechanics are called as expert witnesses. Defending a drug-possession charge, I once retained a Volvo mechanic to testify about the interior of a 1983 Volvo so the jury could see that it was impossible for the police officer, looking through the passenger window, to have seen the defendant's hands reaching under the driver's seat. Because the original car could not be located, the mechanic was also used to lay the foundation for pictures that were taken by my investigator in a salvage yard of a 1983 Volvo.

When an issue arises involving the value of certain property alleged to be damaged or destroyed, an appraiser is often called as an expert to give an opinion regarding the described property's value.

In cases involving securities fraud, a broker or a financial manager is often called to testify about the standards among the industry in order to establish that the defendant was or was not acting in accordance with industry standards.

WILL THE EXPERT BE HELPFUL?

The key to calling an expert witness is that his testimony must be helpful to the jury. And the expert may not render an opinion on the ultimate issue before the jury. Both of these principles are well rooted in the Federal Rules of Evidence.

For example:

▶ You may not call an expert to testify that a witness is lying. Truth and veracity are issues for the jury to decide.

▶ If a defendant charged with first-degree murder is pursuing a lesser-degree offense of voluntary manslaughter, the court will likely refuse to let a psychiatrist testify that the defendant acted "in the heat of passion" during the killing. The issue of "heat of passion" versus intentional, premeditated murder is an issue for the jury to decide.

▶ It would probably not be helpful to retain a mechanic or meteorologist to explain the effect of an ice-packed road on a motor vehicle. Such knowledge is more than likely within the common knowledge and understanding of the jury.

In determining if an expert's services are necessary, ask yourself the following questions:

▶ Is the issue you intend to have the expert witness address relevant to the defendant's theory of the case?

▶ Is the issue outside the common knowledge and understanding of the jury such that expert testimony is required?

▶ Will the prosecution call an expert on an issue to prove its theory of the case? (This should be apparent from the reports provided to you during the discovery process and from the witnesses the prosecution has endorsed to testify at trial.)

▶ Can the prosecution's expert be utilized to educate the jury on the defense issue?

▶ What type of expert will be relevant and helpful?

▶ What is the cost of this type of expert?

▶ Can the defense afford the expert's fees?

To illustrate, imagine that you are trying a first-degree murder case. Your theory of the case concedes that the defendant committed the crime, but in the heat of passion as opposed to with premeditation. The defendant was under extreme stress at the time of the murder because the victim had molested the defendant's daughter and was acquitted of the crime at a jury trial.

The defense theory of the case proposes that at the time of the murder, the victim taunted the defendant about the molestation acquittal and, therefore, the defendant killed in the heat of passion. Certain eyewitness statements suggest that the victim was laughing at and pointing to the defendant just before the murder. Your defense claims that this is circumstantial evidence to corroborate the claim of taunting.

The defendant maintains that he does not remember the killing.

In presenting this theory of the case, you may want to retain a psychological expert to examine the defendant and to render an opinion that gives some psychological reason why the defendant cannot remember the killing.

In applying the above series of questions to this scenario, the answers would be as follows:

▶ *Is the expert testimony on a particular issue relevant to the defendant's theory of the case?* Yes. Explaining the defendant's lack of memory of the killings is relevant to the defendant's theory of the case. The lack of memory may be too convenient in the eyes of the jury; the expert will help explain to them why the defendant contends he cannot remember the killing.

▶ *Is the issue outside the common knowledge and understanding of the jury such that expert testimony is required?* Yes. Lack of memory due to some psychological disorder is more than likely outside the common knowledge and understanding of the jury.

▶ *Will the prosecutor call an expert on the issue to prove his theory of the case?* Probably not. The fact that the defendant contends that he cannot remember the killing is a "good fact" for the prosecution, and there is no direct evidence to support the defendant's claim of "taunting." The prosecution will argue that the taunting never occurred and the defendant's lack of memory is just a convenient, self-serving statement.

The prosecution may retain an expert to evaluate and render an opinion about the defendant's emotional well-being only after the defense has proffered its own expert report supporting the defense theory of the case. (In most jurisdictions, expert reports intended to be relied upon by the defense must be disclosed and turned over to the prosecution before trial.)

▶ *Can the prosecution's expert be utilized to educate the jury on the defense issue?* The prosecutor is unlikely to call an expert in this issue. In some cases, however, the prosecution will have an expert who can be utilized to educate the jury on your alternative theory. For example, if fingerprints at a crime scene were analyzed by the state's latent fingerprint examiner and found to belong to someone other than the defendant, then you may want to call this examiner in your case to testify to this fact. In this instance, you spend no money except for the cost of preparing and serving the subpoena.

However, beware of a latent print examiner who examines prints left at a scene and renders the opinion that the prints are "not comparable." What this means in "prosecutor speak" is that the prints do not have enough identifiable points of interest to be compared to any known prints. The well-coached latent print examiner will testify that the prints could still belong to the defendant, but that there are simply not enough identifiable points to make a comparison within a reasonable degree of certainty.

▶ *What type of expert will be relevant and helpful?* You should always engage a psychological expert when dealing with the defendant's state of mind. You should also engage a psychological expert who will observe and interview the defendant and then conduct standardized tests to support her findings. (There are at least two national standardized written tests that can be conducted. The tests have questions built in that enable the examiners/graders to determine the validity of the examinee's results.)

▶ *What is the cost of this type of expert and can the defendant afford it?* Always know what you can afford before beginning to engage experts to examine the case. If the state is paying for the cost of the defense, as is often the case in homicides, cost becomes a major factor.

In the world of criminal defense experts, you often get what you pay for. In other words, if you hire an expert because she is the cheapest in the market, her cost may often be reflected in the quality or veracity of her testimony.

FINDING EXPERT WITNESSES

Experts are not often found in the yellow pages. Attorneys have to get pretty creative in finding them. I find the following places helpful:

▶ *Ask fellow attorneys.* Ask if they have ever dealt with the issue and retained an expert regarding the same. Just as with legal research and writing, someone out there has already done the work to find a similar expert.

▶ *Consult your local bar associations.* Various attorney organizations maintain databases on experts who can be retained for various subjects. These databases may even contain favorable or unfavorable commentary from the attorney who retained the services of the expert. The Colorado Criminal Defense Bar, of which I am a member, has an Internet list service through which all of the members communicate and share information. I have been successful on numerous occasions in soliciting the names of potential expert witnesses from the wonderful members of this group.

▶ *Contact the authors of relevant articles and treatises.* The Internet, Westlaw, Lexus-Nexis, a local law school library, a local bar or court library, or even a local public library will contain vast numbers of periodicals, books, or treatises on the subject at issue. If the resource is particularly helpful and well-written, contact the author and see if he can assist you. These works often contain the author's credentials and may include his contact information. Just like lawyers, experts write articles to broaden their credentials and curriculum vitas, or to obtain tenure. They are often open to reviewing your case for the same reasons.

▶ *Ask for referrals from experts who turn you down.* If an expert cannot help, they may direct you to a colleague or someone else who may be helpful.

▶ *Attend CLEs or conferences addressing the subject.* Often, criminal science experts are presenters at criminal law conferences. The conference presentation materials may contain names of experts or lead you to resources in which you may find experts.

▶ *Consult local professional organizations.* There is more than likely a local professional organization whose members have the specialized knowledge that you need. For example, the American Medical Association has an Internet site that lists virtually every physician in every specialty in the country, along with the physician's contact information. Should you need a financial expert, contact the local CPA organization or brokerage association.

▶ *Ask at local universities.* Universities have chemists, physicists, engineers, linguists, sociologists, and other scientists who may be available to give an expert opinion. For example, a sociology professor with expertise in cultural studies may be helpful if you have an issue regarding the conduct of a defendant that can be explained by cultural practice.

► *Review prominent cases that have involved the same issues.* If I cannot find experts any other way, I like to steal them. Reviewing the court case files addressing similar issues can be helpful. The files may contain the names of both defense and prosecution experts. The expert's field of expertise and contact information may appear in an endorsement of witnesses. The expert's opinions and contact information may also appear in a motion in limine in which one side seeks to exclude the testimony of the expert at trial.

I once heard about a good expert who was utilized by a local attorney to discredit the prosecution's breath-test results in DUI cases. When persistent inquiries to the attorney regarding the expert's name failed, I went to the court clerk's office and looked through several DUI files in which the defense attorney had appeared until I found the name of the expert.

► *As a last resort, look for experts who advertise in bar journals.* The problem with these experts is that they have made a career out of providing trial testimony. They have no other real job in their field of expertise. Experts who make a career out of testifying are often portrayed to the jury as someone who will say anything to earn their fees.

OUTLINE YOUR CROSS-EXAMINATION AND DIRECT EXAMINATION

Cross-Examinations

Always begin by outlining your cross-examinations. I say this because trials are won by the defense on cross-examination. Since the defense never has the burden of proof, cross-examination is the stage on which the defense presents its theory of the case and demonstrates to the jury that the prosecution's case leaves reasonable doubt about the defendant's guilt.

The cross-examination should flow easily and fall into place if you have prepared the "Good Fact/Bad Fact" list and a defense theory of the case as previously discussed.

A sample Cross-Examination Outline is included as Exhibit LL on the enclosed CD-ROM. ↝

TIPS FOR CROSS-EXAMINING

1. *Write down the precise points you want to make, but do not script questions.* Scripted questions can inhibit your ability to deviate from the outline or

your theory of the case. Witnesses often raise points that you may not have intended to address until later; a well-prepared attorney can easily deviate from the outline and address the point, then return right back to the order of her outline.

2. *Annotate your facts.* Note where the fact can be located in the discovery, which witness will testify or has testified consistently with the fact, or which exhibit establishes the fact. Should a witness change his story or give an answer that contradicts the facts, you can immediately impeach the witness or refresh his recollection.

3. *Avoid making more than one point at a time.* Do not ask compound questions, such as, "This event occurred in the morning, on February 23, 2003, when you were on your way to work?" This question addresses three separate facts: the event occurred in the morning; the event occurred on February 23, 2003; and the event occurred as the witness was on his way to work. Rather, you should ask one question per question:

Defense Counsel: You say this event occurred in the morning?

Witness: Yes.

Defense Counsel: At the time, you were on your way to work?

Witness: Yes.

Defense Counsel: And the date this event occurred was February 23, 2003?

Witness: Yes.

4. *Outline your points following the theory of recency and primacy.*

   ▼ Your second most important point should be the first point you make.

   ▼ Your most important point should be your last point.

Juries remember less than 20 percent of the points you make. And, for some reason, they tend to recall the first point and the last point that you make on cross-examination. If you bury your best point in the middle of your cross-examination, you are lessening your chances that the point will have an impact on the jurors.

5. *Never ask a question to which you do not know the answer.* The exception is if the answer does not really matter, or if you are asking a rhetorical question to make a point to the jury, as in, "Mr. Smith, you're trying to get Mr. Defendant convicted, aren't you?"

6. *Know when not to cross-examine a witness.* It is sometimes best to skip cross-examination of witnesses who neither help nor hurt your case.

   ▼ If you attempt to cross-examine such a witness, you may accidentally open an issue that hurts your case.

▼ Skipping a cross-examination may lead the jury to believe that the witness had nothing important to say, and they may dismiss the testimony he gave on direct.

Sometimes a witness's testimony will not hurt your case.
It may be merely foundational.
The witness may be used to introduce evidence that you do not contest.
The witness may be used to set the scene or explain why the investigating officers took some action.
Much of this falls under the theory of never asking a witness a question to which you do not know the answer.

Direct Examinations

Outline your direct examination after outlining your cross-examination, following the same rules and tips. As with your cross-examination, your direct examination will flow easily and fall into place if you have prepared the "Good Fact/Bad Fact" list and a defense theory of the case.

Questions raised on direct examination should be open-ended and should not be leading (in order to avoid having the question and answer struck). For your first few trials, you may want to script these questions in order to word them in such a way as to elicit a particular response. This is because it is a lot harder to elicit the answer you want on direct without leading the witness. The witness cannot read your mind and may find it difficult to follow your questions and give you the desired response. If you think through your questions, you can develop a question with the precise wording that may more effectively elicit the response you need without leading the witness.

However, once you get the hang of it, you should stop scripting your questions. As in cross-examination, rigidly scripted questions can inhibit your ability to deviate from and quickly return to your outline.

A sample Direct Examination Outline is included as Exhibit MM on the enclosed CD-ROM. ➙

OUTLINE YOUR OPENING STATEMENT AND CLOSING ARGUMENT

Opening Statement

A good attorney always prepares his opening statement in advance. I subscribe to the following rules in preparing my opening statements:

▶ *The opening should flow like a story.* Presenting your opening like a story allows you to present certain points in an argumentative manner without drawing an objection. Should the court sustain the prosecutor's objection that you are being argumentative in your opening statement, add the statement, "The evidence will show . . ." and then continue on with your story until you draw another sustained objection for being argumentative.

▶ *Begin and end with the theory of the case.* For example, begin by telling the jury, "Mr. Defendant did not commit this crime. Someone else committed this crime." End by telling the jury, ". . . and at the end of all of the evidence in this case, I am going to ask you to find that Mr. Defendant is not guilty of committing this crime."

▶ *Draft your opening outline using your "Good Facts/Bad Facts" list.* Focus on the facts that are good for you and that can later by applied by the jury to the law which the court instructs them to consider. Use the good facts to tell the defendant's story; explain away bad facts if absolutely necessary for the jury to accept your theory of the case.

▶ *Make your most important points first and last* (the theory of recency and primacy).

▶ *Generalize your facts* to avoid being boxed in to a particular position that could be discredited by the prosecution. If you state something for a fact in the opening statement and the prosecution later discredits it, you will appear untrustworthy to the jury.

This last point is well illustrated by a burglary case I once tried. My theory of the case was that defendant came upon the house already burglarized. The defendant claimed he had entered the house to check on the welfare of the owner, whom the defendant claimed he knew. Finding the house empty, the defendant left to call a friend, then came back and waited in the house for either the owner to arrive home or his friend to come pick him up. When the owner arrived home, he found the defendant and the friend in his burglarized house.

In order to tell my client's story, I had to explain in opening statement why my client was in a home he did not burglarize and why his friend was there with him. In order to tell my client's story, I had to explain some bad facts: why he was in the burglarized house and why his friend was with him. My opening statement, based upon information revealed to me by the defendant, detailed that after having come upon the burglarized home, the defendant "walked four blocks up to Broadway Street" and paged a friend from the "pay phone in front of the laundromat." The friend "called my client back on the pay phone." It was during this return call, I told the jury, that the defendant asked the friend to come pick him up at the victim's house.

Immediately after opening statements, the investigating officer spoke to the prosecutor and then left the courtroom. Later, the prosecutor called the officer to testify that he checked on the pay telephone I had described, the only one in front of a laundromat on Broadway, four blocks from the victim's house—and that this pay phone did not receive incoming telephone calls. Of course, this completely discredited me and my client.

What should I have done? I should have told the jury simply that the defendant left the house briefly to call a friend, and the friend met defendant at the burglarized house to pick him up. I should not have told the jury the defendant walked four blocks. I should not have told the jury he walked to Broadway Street. I should not have told the jury he called from a pay phone. I should not have told the jury the defendant received a return call from the friend on the pay phone. I should not have told the jury where the pay phone was.

When I described the pay phone, the investigating officer was in the courtroom as the prosecutor's consulting witness. He knew the area quite well as it was his beat. He also happened to know that to control the prostitution traffic in the neighborhood, this phone had been disabled from receiving incoming calls. The prosecutor later told me that the phone would have been a nonissue had I not described it with such specificity and piqued the investigating officer's interest.

Closing Argument

Closing argument is your opportunity to argue the facts and apply them to the law in which the court will instruct the jury. Your job is to convince the jury that the prosecutor has not met his burden of proof. I subscribe to the following rules, many of which will be familiar to you by now, in preparing my closing arguments:

- ► Never script the closing argument—always outline it.
- ► Draft the closing outline using your "Good Facts/Bad Facts" list.
  - ▼ Use the good facts to tell the defendant's story and explain away the bad facts with good facts if you find it necessary.
  - ▼ Highlight only the bad facts that are absolutely necessary to explain away in order for the jury to accept your theory of the case.
- ► Begin and end by telling the jury that the defendant is "not guilty." For example, begin by telling the jury, "Mr. Defendant is not guilty. Someone else committed this crime. . . ." End by telling the jury, "When you go back into that jury room and deliberate the facts of this case, find Mr. Defendant not guilty of committing this crime."
- ► Make your most important points first and last (the theory of recency and primacy).

A sample Closing Statement Outline is included as Exhibit NN on the enclosed CD-ROM. ⬦

DRAFT PROPOSED JURY INSTRUCTIONS

At the close of all trial evidence, the judge will instruct the jury on the law to be applied to the facts of the case. These instructions are called the "jury instructions." Some jurisdictions refer to this as the "jury charge." The prosecution will want the jury instructed in terms that are the most prejudicial to the defense theory of the case. Similarly, the defense attorney desires to have the jury instructed in terms that are most prejudicial to the prosecution theory of the case and most beneficial to the defense theory of the case.

As a defense lawyer, it is your duty to guide the judge to the law on which you believe the jury should be instructed. As such, you should always prepare a list of proposed instructions to be given to the jury. You do not invent the wording of the proposed instructions. The wording of these proposed instructions often comes from the following sources:

▶ *Pattern instructions.* Most jurisdictions have compilations of form instructions that have been developed, drafted, redrafted, tested, and fine-tuned by the appellate courts or the local Criminal Jury Instruction Committee. The instructions, which include the law on affirmative offenses, the duty or function of judge and jury, the burden of proof, the credibility of witnesses, evidentiary issues, culpability and accountability, and the elements of proof for every crime are compiled and published by the major legal publishing houses. You can and should purchase a copy of your jurisdiction's pattern instructions. Should your jurisdiction not have a pattern instruction for a point of law, look to the federal pattern instructions. In jurisdictions that employ pattern criminal instructions, the appellate courts heavily scrutinize trial courts who fail to instruct the jury using these instructions.

▶ *Caselaw.* If the jurisdiction has no pattern instructions, there is no pattern instruction available for a particular issue, or the caselaw has modified the law as reflected in the pattern instructions, go to the caselaw defining the particular issue and draft your own instruction using the wording as exactly as you are able.

PREPARE A TRIAL NOTEBOOK

Good trial attorneys always use trial notebooks in trial. They are an easy and efficient way to organize your trial materials. My trial notebooks consist of one or more 3.5" or 4" quality three-ring binders. All trial materials are hole-punched and placed in the binders, with tabs identifying the documents to be found there. I usually organize my trial notebooks with the following headings and in the following order:

▶ *Complaint and Information.* All charging documents should be kept separate for quick reference.

▶ *Affidavit of probable cause to arrest.* This is an affidavit prepared by the lead investigator in the case, and it is a general allegation of the facts upon which the state bases the charges against the defendant. This document is initially prepared for the court to review and find probable cause to charge and arrest the defendant. The prosecution often uses this affidavit to prepare its own theory of the case.

▶ *Pleadings.* Anything prepared for the court's review and that is filed with the court is a pleading. This includes, for example, motions, orders, subpoenas, and bills of particular.

▶ *Witness lists.* Prepare an alphabetical list of the witnesses you will call, the witnesses endorsed by the prosecution (listed by the prosecutor in the Complaint and Information and in a formal Notice to Endorse additional witnesses), and those named in the discovery. Next to the names of the witnesses, note the facts that may be introduced through their testimony. This is for your use only and should not be given to the prosecutor.

Often, the court will require the prosecutor to prepare a list of witnesses the prosecution intends to call during trial so the court can keep track of the pace of the trial. As you are entitled to a copy of whatever the prosecutor gives to the judge, insist on your own copy of this list and include it in your notebook.

▶ *Exhibit lists.* Prepare an alphabetical list of all exhibits that might be introduced by the prosecution or the defense. This is for your use only and should not be given to the prosecutor.

The prosecution may prepare a list of exhibits to be given to the court and the court reporter in order to track the identification, offering, and admission of the prosecutor's exhibits. Insist on your own copy of this list and include it in your notebook.

▶ *Voir dire questions.*

▶ *Outlines of opening statement and closing argument.*

▶ *Good Facts/Bad Facts list.*

▶ *Notes.* Every note not categorized elsewhere should go here: crude drawings of the crime scene, for example, or notes taken during the interview of a witness or during any previous hearings.

▶ *Correspondence with the prosecution.* Include everything that is not a note, pleading, complaint, report, or outline, e.g., all phone messages and correspondence between you and the prosecution. This is important should an issue arise regarding the nature of an agreement between the parties, or if there is discovery dispute, or if there is a dispute with the client regarding the theory of the defense.

▶ *Police reports.* Keep a complete copy of unedited police reports here. This is important if a discovery violation issue arises. This enables you to show the court the complete set of discovery you have received from the prosecution.

▶ *Expert reports.*

▶ *Cross-examination outline.* Include extra copies of reports that can be readily used to impeach or refresh a witness on the point you are trying to make with your cross-examination.

▶ *Direct examination outline.* Again, include extra copies of reports that can be readily used to impeach or refresh a witness on the point you are trying to make with your direct examination.

▶ *Research.* Have copies of case law or treatises regarding the admission of certain evidence, the exclusion of certain evidence, and the burden of proof for the prosecutor's claims.

▶ *Proposed jury instructions.*

CHAPTER 9

Trying the Case

VOIR DIRE

Voir dire is the process of questioning the jury panel by the attorneys, and sometimes the court, in order to discover the backgrounds, predispositions, and biases of the potential jurors. The various experiences and preexisting notions of the potential jurors reflect on their ability to be fair and impartial in judging the case.

The information obtained during voir dire enables the parties to determine whom to strike from the panel. The panel can be questioned as a group, or individuals may be questioned one-on-one. It all depends on the court's preference. The panel may be required to answer a jury questionnaire in advance of the trial. The questionnaires may be standard questionnaires prepared by the court, or the court might invite the parties to submit questions to be included in the questionnaires. Sometimes, when questionnaires are not the court's standard protocol, defense attorneys motion the court to submit a questionnaire to the jury. You may be given some time by the court to obtain copies of the questionnaire answers from the jury clerk or the judge's clerk and to review the answers in advance of voir dire. (I have received these the morning of trial and as much as two days in advance of trial.)

Prosecution's Voir Dire

As with every other part of the trial, the prosecutor begins his voir dire first.

All prosecutors are trained that persuasion and education are the goals of voir dire. They attempt to educate and indoctrinate the jury about the prosecution's theory of the case. They attempt to define the law and get the jury to agree to the prosecution's interpretation of the law. In doing so, they try to minimize their burden of proof.

The following example is something I have heard prosecutors say in voir dire in order to minimize their burden of proof:

117

Now, ladies and gentlemen, my burden of proof is to prove the defendant's doubt beyond all reasonable doubt. But this does not mean that I have to prove his guilt beyond a shadow of a doubt or beyond all doubt.

Now, will anybody here hold me to a burden of proof beyond all doubt or beyond a shadow of a doubt?

Defense Voir Dire

I often find voir dire to be the most difficult part of the trial. The time allotted by the judge is never enough time for me to indoctrinate, educate, or persuade the jury to the defense theory of the case.

According to Bert Nieslanik, a very accomplished trial attorney (he is the present director of the Colorado Alternate Defense Counsel's postconviction division and an instructor at the National Criminal Defense College and the Western Trial Advocacy Institute, among other programs), you should accomplish three things during voir dire:

► Get the jury to like you;

► Get the jury to trust you;

► Entertain the jury.

I would add: Determine the potential jurors' predispositions and biases toward the defendant and your theory of the case by their responses to your voir dire questions.

Subjects to Address with Potential Jurors

The following is a noninclusive list of topics to discuss with the potential jurors during voir dire to help determine the juror's predispositions, biases, and general fitness to sit as a juror:

► Physical conditions that may inhibit a juror's ability to serve

  ▼ Physical discomfort in sitting through a trial

  ▼ Special type of machine for maintaining health

  ▼ Problems with vision or hearing

What this may tell you: You want jurors that can give their full attention to the evidence, especially your cross-examination and theory of the case. Jurors with certain physical conditions or health problems may not be able to give the case their full attention. The court will often allow jurors with certain physical conditions to be relieved from jury duty for cause.

► Prior jury service

  ▼ Type of case: criminal, civil, or court martial

  ▼ Was the potential juror the foreman?

▼ Was a verdict reached?

▼ Was it an enjoyable experience?

What this may tell you: Prior jury service in a case that went to verdict may tell you good things or bad things about the potential juror.

▼ The potential juror knows how the process works and, especially, the inner workings of the deliberation process. He may keep the other jurors in line and keep them focused on the instructions of the law.

▼ If the potential juror once served on a civil jury, which does not have to render a unanimous verdict, he may ignore or misinterpret the instructions regarding a unanimous verdict and persuade fellow jurors to follow suit. Also, the burden of proof in civil cases is much lower than proof beyond a reasonable doubt; this juror may ignore or misinterpret the instructions regarding proof beyond a reasonable doubt and persuade fellow jurors to follow suit.

▼ If the potential juror has previously been a jury foreman, chances are good that he will be elected as the foreman in this case, or at least be a leader of the group. If you like how he responds to other voir dire questions, then keep him on the jury, because he may help you persuade other jurors to your theory of the case. If you do not like how he responds to other voir dire questions, then strike him so that he does not have the opportunity to persuade other jurors against your theory of the case.

▼ If the potential juror did not enjoy his previous jury experience, then chances are good he will not enjoy serving as a juror on your case. You want the jurors to give you their full attention, and a person that did not enjoy his previous jury experience may not give your case appropriate attention.

► Knowledge of the parties

▼ know defendant or his family

▼ know defense attorney or her firm

▼ know prosecution attorney or anyone in his office

What this may tell you: Everybody has biases and predispositions. If a potential juror indicates she knows you, someone involved in the case, or someone related to someone else who is involved in the case, you should assume she has formed an opinion about whomever she knows. This opinion may affect how she views the evidence.

► Knowledge of any of the potential witnesses to be called by the state or defense

What this may tell you: This may affect how he views the witness's testimony.

▶ Knowledge of any other potential juror

What this may tell you: Most people are followers. If jurors know one another, one may feel inclined to follow the lead of the other; or even worse, try to impress the other. You want your jurors to be independent and open-minded, and able to stand their ground when their opinions differ from others.

▶ Marital status

What this may tell you: Married people are sometimes better at compromise than single people. This could be good or bad for you, depending upon your theory of the case.

▶ Employment

What this may tell you: A person's employment can often tell you how they will view the evidence. For instance, an engineer or accountant will be meticulous and require some logical order as to how the facts of the case fit together. This could be good or bad for you, depending upon your theory of the case.

▶ Spouse's employment

What this may tell you: Often, people know a lot about their spouse's work. They may have formed opinions about the job and consider themselves knowledgeable about the subject area. This could be good or bad for you, depending upon your theory of the case.

▶ Children

What this may tell you:

▼ People who have children believe themselves to be pretty good at detecting truthfulness.

▼ You may desire mothers on your jury panel if you have a very young and sympathetic client.

▶ Crime victims or advocates

▼ family or self

▼ is there a type of case that the potential juror would not be a good juror for

▼ involved in a group or organization that advocates a change in laws regarding crime or violence

What this may tell you:

▼ If your case involves a crime of violence (assault, rape, kidnapping, murder, etc.), it will be very hard for a potential juror who has been or is closely related to someone who has been a victim of a crime of violence to set aside any bias or predisposition that the potential juror may have toward crime and criminal defendants' rights under the justice system.

▼ If a potential juror is involved in a group or organization that advocates more severe criminal laws, then that person probably believes that the criminal justice system is too lenient toward criminal defendants. This potential juror will have a bias against criminal defendants, and you should assume it will be unfavorable to your client during the deliberation process.

▶ Any relation to law enforcement

   ▼ self

   ▼ family member

   ▼ close friend

What this may tell you: Some people, based on personal experience or experiences shared with them by others, believe that law enforcement officers are incapable of fault. If you intend to be critical of law enforcement officers as part of your theory of defense, determine if a potential juror may be offended by your attack on law enforcement.

▶ Presumption of innocence

   ▼ Explain the concept and ask if anyone has difficulty with it.

   ▼ Determine if the potential jurors can presume the defendant's innocence until they have heard all of the evidence and arguments and until they are convinced beyond a reasonable doubt.

What this may tell you: If a potential juror has a difficulty accepting this concept, then you may want to have her stricken from the jury. You should be suspect of anyone who does not believe or has difficulty grasping that a criminal defendant is presumed innocent.

How this may help you: This may help you educate the jury about the need to listen to every fact and consider every fact and lack thereof, before they make a determination as to defendant's guilt. It may prevent a circumstance in which a juror decides, during the course of the prosecution's case-in-chief, that she has heard enough evidence and is convinced of the defendant's guilt and refuses to pay attention to further evidence or argument.

▶ Burden of proof

   ▼ proof beyond all reasonable doubt

   ▼ If prosecution is allowed to define doubt in his voir dire as meaning not beyond all doubt, make clear that the only doubt the jury can have is an unreasonable doubt.

Give the jurors an example of a reasonable doubt and an unreasonable doubt. For example, an unreasonable doubt may be a doubt as to whether the defendant was present when the crime was committed because the juror believes space aliens actually committed the crime.

▼ make it clear that the burden never shifts to the defendant

▼ defendant is never required to testify

▼ defendant is never required to present any evidence

▼ defendant is never required to prove that he is not guilty

What this may tell you: If potential jurors have difficulty accepting these concepts, then you may want to have them stricken from the jury. You should be suspect of anyone who does not believe or has difficulty grasping that a criminal defendant is presumed innocent.

How this may help you: This may help you educate the jury about the fact that they need to hold the prosecutor to a higher standard than the defense. It may prevent a circumstance in which a juror decides, during the course of the trial or deliberation, that the defendant is guilty because he failed to present any proof as to his innocence; or that defendant is guilty because he did not testify on his own behalf.

► Been to court for any reason whatsoever (other than those already discussed)

▼ criminal matter

▼ civil matter

▼ divorce

▼ child custody

▼ adoption

▼ witness

▼ moral support for friend or family

▼ how was the experience

What this may tell you: If a potential juror has any previous involvement with the judicial system, then she probably has an opinion about how the system works. The potential juror may consider herself so knowledgeable about the law and how the system works that she does not pay attention to the law as instructed by the judge. Again, this could be good or bad for the defense, depending upon the defense theory of the case. The potential juror may also have a bias for or against a party because of her previous experience with the judicial system.

► Any reason whatsoever why a potential juror could not be fair and impartial

What this may tell you: Potential jurors who may have a bias do not always come out and say they cannot be fair and impartial in response to other questions. You will be surprised how often this question gets a response from potential jurors. If the juror answers your question in the affirmative, then you would be well advised to strike him.

Whatever response a potential juror gives to each of these question topics, it is important to follow up with a question pertaining to whether the particular position or belief will affect the juror's ability to be fair and impartial.

PICKING THE JURY

After voir dire, each party is allowed to strike a certain number of potential jurors from the venire panel (the list of potential jurors summoned to serve as potential jurors for a particular term) in order to arrive at the ultimate jury panel.

The term "picking the jury" is a misnomer since the process actually involves eliminating potential jurors in order to reduce the panel to a group of individuals who, in the attorney's mind, are the least likely to be unfair to his side.

A party may strike a potential juror from the jury panel for cause or exercise a peremptory strike.

Strikes for Cause

Either during voir dire or directly thereafter the court will ask either side if it desires to strike certain individuals for cause. To strike a potential juror for cause means to remove the potential juror from the panel for reasons that law and public policy recognize as sufficient warrant for removal. In other words, the potential juror cannot be removed on grounds that are arbitrary and capricious.

Grounds for cause are usually defined by local statute or local case, or both. The trial court has the ultimate discretion whether to allow a party to strike a potential juror for cause. The court's decision can be overturned on appeal only if the court is found to have abused its discretion and that abuse prejudiced the defendant in his right to a fair trial.

As many people as necessary can be struck for cause, and these strikes do not affect the number of peremptory strikes given to either side.

Grounds to strike for cause may include

▶ Relationship to the parties
▶ Intimate knowledge of the case

▶ Preexisting commitments

▶ Health problems

The court will sometimes give the parties a list of people that the court believes should be let go for cause. (The court may get the information establishing the grounds for cause from answers to jury questionnaires or in voir dire, or from jurors who approached the court outside the presence of other jurors.) Thereafter, the court gives the attorneys an opportunity to object and make argument outside the presence of the jury.

It is always best to find a reason to strike a potential juror for cause rather than waste a peremptory challenge to strike the potential juror.

Peremptory Strikes

Depending upon the severity level of the crime, each party is given a predetermined number of peremptory strikes. Each party can use these strikes to strike an individual for any reason other than race or gender, without having to give a reason for the strike to the court or other party.

The parties take turns making their strikes. The prosecution makes the first strike.

Some courts allow this to be accomplished outside the presence of the jury and some require you to make your strikes aloud, in front of the entire potential jury panel.

Exercising Your Peremptory Strikes

Many of the potential jurors will be given a number. They will be assigned a seating order and be required to sit in the same seat throughout the entire voir dire process. The idea is that the jurors in the chairs number numbered 1 through 12 (if it is a 12-person jury) will make up the final jury.

Should either side strike a potential juror in seat 1 through 12, then the remaining 11 will move forward, with the last spot to be filled by the next potential juror who was present during voir dire. (Sometimes the jurors will remain in their seats and the empty spot will be filled by the new potential juror.) Thus, in making peremptory strikes, it is important to focus on the first 12 chairs that reflect the number of jurors (and potentially alternate jurors) that will make up the panel.

Batson *Challenge*

A *Batson* challenge is an objection to a peremptory strike made by either party on the grounds that a potential juror was struck on the basis of race or gender.[1] Unless otherwise specified by the court, you must ask to approach

---

[1] *Batson* challenges come from the decisions of *Batson v. Kentucky*, 476 U.S. 79 (1986), and *Powers v. Ohio*, 499 U.S. 400 (1991).

the judge immediately after the challenged strike is made and allege that the particular individual was struck on the basis of race or gender. The court will require the striking party to articulate a race- or gender-neutral basis for the strike. Should the reason be insufficient, the court will allow the potential juror to serve despite the attempted strike.

OPENING STATEMENT

The opening statement is a statement made to the jury which previews the evidence that the defense believes will be elicited during trial. It focuses upon the facts that will support the defense theory of the case. Because the defense does not have the burden of proof, the defense is allowed to waive the opening statement. Some jurisdictions allow the defense to reserve opening statements until after the prosecution has rested and before the defense puts on its case in chief.

I cannot think of any good reason to waive or reserve opening statement.

Sometimes, the best defense a defendant may have is his attorney and the jury's relationship with that attorney. When given the opportunity to speak to the jury, the defense attorney should always take it. If a jury likes and relates to the defense attorney, it may be hard for them to convict the defendant, no matter how heinous the crime. The jury may believe that there is no way that such a likeable attorney could represent a person guilty of the crime charged.

The following tips may be helpful in presenting your opening statement:

▶ *Begin with the theory of the case.* The first statement that should come out of the defense attorney's mouth in opening statement is the defense theory of the case. Example:

Ladies and gentleman, Joe Smith is not guilty. He could not have committed the crime alleged by the Prosecution. At the time the crime was committed, he was in another town, hours away.

▶ *Tell a story.* The opening should flow like a story. Pretend to be explaining the theory of the case and the facts and evidence that support it to a family member who is not familiar with the law.

▶ *Opening statement do's and don'ts:*

  ▼ Do not begin opening by telling the jury that what you are about to say to them is not evidence.

  ▼ Do not tell the jury that a certain witness will testify in a certain way. (A witness will inevitably say something different than expected and you may not be successful in impeaching that witness.)

▼ Avoid being specific as to how various facts and evidence will reach the jury.

▼ Do not tell the jury that the defense will "prove" anything. Doing so only raises the jurors' expectations against the defendant to prove he is innocent. It unnecessarily shifts the burden to the defense.

▼ Do not use the word "story" when telling them the defendant's story.

▼ Do not script the opening. Make an outline that fits on a couple of pages. Scripting will only make you more nervous, which makes the jury uncomfortable.

▼ Do not highlight the bad facts of the case. Unless you have a good reason to explain them, try not to mention them at all.

▼ Do mention those bad facts that must be explained away in order for the jury to subscribe to the theory of defense.

▼ Do generalize facts so as to avoid being boxed in to a position by the prosecution.

▼ Do end the opening statement by repeating the defense theory of the case.

A sample Opening Statement Transcript is included as Exhibit OO on the enclosed CD-ROM. ▬◆

CROSS-EXAMINATION

The defense case is often won and lost in cross-examination. For cross to be effective, a defense attorney must master the facts as they appear in the discovery. This allows the attorney to smoothly deviate from his cross-examination outline depending upon the response given by the witness.

The following tips may be helpful in conducting your cross-examinations:

Signposting

Begin each area of inquiry for cross by telling the witness (and the jury) the area upon which you desire to question. For example: "Mr. Walker, I want to ask you some questions about what you were doing before you say you witnessed a struggle between Mr. Rodriguez (the defendant) and Mr. McCartney (the victim)."

This helps the witness understand the focus of your question, i.e., you do not discuss what he did between the struggle and before the police arrived, or before he testified, etc.

It also puts the jury in the right frame of mind to say, "A-ha! This is where the witness is going to tell me X as told to me by the defense attorney in opening statement."

Signposting rarely draws an objection, and the few objections against me for doing this were not sustained. Should the prosecution's objection be sustained, however, simply rephrase your statement into a question, e.g., "Mr. Walker, is it okay if I ask you some questions about what you were doing before you say you witnessed a struggle between Mr. Rodriguez and Mr. McCartney?"

Cross-Examination Advice

The following is a noninclusive list of pointers for cross:

► Avoid compound questions.

► Ask only leading questions that call for a "yes" or "no" answer (a leading question is a question that suggests the answer).

► Make your most important points following the theory of recency and primacy.

► Never ask a question to which you do not know the answer, unless the answer does not really matter and you are merely trying to make a point to the jury.

► Do not rehash the bad facts testified to on direct examination by the witness.

► Keep your points as brief and as simple as possible.

► Do not be afraid to skip cross of certain witnesses. Sometimes, everything that the defense needs from a witness has already been said in response to direct exam. Cross-examination may open the door to rehabilitate or rehash issues the defense prefers to avoid.

► Keep a copy of the witness's statements or an officer's report for each witness with your cross-examination outline. In the event the witness cannot remember making a statement or testifies differently from a previous statement, provide him with a copy of his statement or report to refresh his recollection or to impeach him.

Controlling the Witness

Witnesses can play games. They ramble and avoid answering the question to try to make the defense attorney look stupid or the defendant look bad; or they raise inappropriate, prejudicial facts. There are ways for defense counsel to control witnesses and keep them from playing games.

TIPS FOR CONTROLLING THE WITNESS[2]

1. *Maintain eye contact.* Maintain eye contact from the moment the question begins until the witness has finished answering the question. Keep the contact for some time after the witness stops talking (this could be a millisecond). This sends an unspoken message to the witness that "I have my eye on you and I will make a fool of you if you try anything."

2. *Repeat the question.* Should the witness fail to properly answer the question, repeat the question more slowly without breaking eye contact. Should the witness still refuse to answer, ask the question even more slowly, taking care to enunciate every word, all the while without breaking eye contact.

3. *Ask the question in reverse.* Should the witness fail to properly answer the question, repeat the question in the reverse. For example:

   Defense Counsel: The man you saw running down the alley was black?

   Witness: Well, everything happened so fast, the victim got hit with the board, and then he cried out and there were people running everywhere . . . *blah, blah, blah* . . .

   Defense Counsel: The man you saw running down the alley wasn't black?

   Witness: *Blah, blah, blah* . . . no, that's not true.

   Defense Counsel: The man you saw running down the alley was black?

   Witness: Yes.

4. *Use a hand gesture.* An outstretched, open hand, a hand waving in the air, or a wagging finger directed at the witness is highly effective in stopping the witness from running on. I do not know why it works, but it does.

5. *Tell the witness, "Stop."* Interrupting the running-on witness with a "stop" will cause the witness to stop talking. It will also invoke an objection. However, the witness has stopped by then and has forgotten what she was saying. This enables the cross-examiner to ask the question in another way or move the witness along and away from the damaging or nonresponsive statements she is so determined to make.

6. *Ask a series of eliminating questions.* Ask a nonresponsive witness a series of questions that eliminate all other facts except the one that you are trying to elicit from the witness. For example:

   Defense Counsel: The man you saw running down the alley was black?

---

[2]Adapted from Larry Pozner and Roger Dodd, *Controlling the Runaway Witness: Tried & True Techniques for Cross-Examination,* TRIAL (January 1991). Another excellent resource is POZNER & DODD, CROSS EXAMINATION: SCIENCE & TECHNIQUES (2nd ed. 1993).

Witness: Well, everything happened so fast, the victim got hit with the board, and then he cried out and there were people running everywhere . . . *blah, blah, blah* . . .

Defense Counsel: The man you saw running down the alley was white?

Witness: *Blah, blah, blah* . . . no, that's not true.

Defense Counsel: The man was Latino?

Witness: No.

Defense Counsel: The man was black?

Witness: No.

Defense Counsel: The man was Asian?

Witness: No.

Defense Counsel: The man you saw was white?

Witness: Yes.

MOTIONS FOR JUDGMENT OF ACQUITTAL

Immediately after the prosecution rests its case in chief, make an oral motion for a Judgment of Acquittal. This motion asks the court to acquit the defendant based upon the evidence presented by the prosecution.

In order to grant the motion, the court must find that, in viewing the evidence in the light most favorable to the prosecution, no reasonable jury could convict the defendant on the charges.

DIRECT EXAMINATION

Direct examination involves presenting testimony and evidence by calling witnesses. The object is to question the witnesses in a manner that tells a story; preferably a story that relates to the defense theory of the case.

Often, the defense does not present evidence in this manner. That is because the defense is not required to present any evidence. The prosecution has the burden of proof, which never shifts to the defense. If the defense does present evidence, it is usually through cross-examination of the prosecution's witnesses. As such, direct examinations can be difficult and cumbersome for defense attorneys. In essence, we lack practice because we do not do it often enough.

Unlike cross-examination, in direct the examiner is not allowed to lead the witness (unless the witness is hostile to the defense). This makes it difficult to begin and end your examination with your best points. This is because the witness must be directed in a way that tells a story that is easy for the jury to follow.

Decision to Call Witnesses

DEFENDANT

The defendant has a right to testify on his own behalf. He can testify regardless of your advice. His testimony is presented through direct examination.

Some defense attorneys believe that you should always talk the defendant out of taking the stand. They believe that a defendant is never a good witness for himself. I think, perhaps, that some of these attorneys are not good at conducting direct examination. I have won many cases by calling my client to the stand. Often, the defendant is the only witness to his story.

The decision to advise the defendant to take the stand and testify in his own defense can be difficult. Some defendants are not very intelligent or articulate. They may not understand your questions on direct examination and may be easily confused and trapped by the prosecutor's questions on cross-examination. But if your theory of the case involves evidence that can be presented only through the defendant's testimony, then you have no choice but to call your client to the stand, if he is willing to testify.

OTHER WITNESSES

Consider these four principles in calling witnesses to testify in the defense case-in-chief:

▶ The witness's testimony must be helpful to the defense theory of the case.

▶ The evidence that will be presented through the witness's testimony should involve an issue that was not addressed or raised through cross-examination of the prosecutor's witnesses.

▶ The importance of the testimony you intend to obtain from the witness must outweigh any negative evidence that can be elicited from the witness by the prosecutor on cross-examination.

▶ You must be able to address, impeach, or explain away any negative information that is elicited from the witness by the prosecutor on cross-examination.

TIPS FOR CONDUCTING DIRECT EXAMINATION

1. *Signpost.* Tell the witness the subject that you would like question him about.

2. *Keep your questions simple.* Ask your question in a manner that elicits a response involving one fact or incident.

3. *Avoid compound questions.* Ask your questions about one fact at a time.

4. *Do not ask leading questions.* Try not to ask leading questions in order to avoid unnecessary objections. Leading questions are not permitted on cross-examination unless the court determines the witness is hostile to the defense.

5. *Do not practice the witness's testimony beforehand.* It is okay to review the subjects that you wish to cover with the witness and the expected answers, just avoid rehearsing your entire direct examination with the witness. Juries are very good at spotting rehearsed testimony. And, although they do not seem to mind rehearsed prosecution witnesses, they are very distrustful of defense witnesses that they believe to be rehearsed.

6. *Keep a copy of the witness's statements or an officer's report for each witness with your direct outline.* In the event the witness cannot remember a fact, provide him with a copy of his statement or report to review and perhaps refresh his recollection.

7. *Avoid "What happened" and "Then what happened" questions.* Too often, the prosecution will conduct direct examinations in this manner. Each answer to a question is followed by the question, "And then what happened?" or "What happened next?" Do not do this. First, it makes you look like the prosecutor. Second, it inhibits your ability to tell a smooth, coherent story with the witness.

Sample Direct Examination

Begin with a signpost: "Mr. Witness, I want you to remember back to the evening of November 2, 2003."

Then, paint a picture for the witness and the jury with your questions:

▶ Do you remember what you were doing that night?

▶ Did there come a time when you observed a confrontation between Mr. McCartney and Mr. Defendant?

▶ Do you remember what you were doing at that moment?

▶ Do you recall what drew your attention to the confrontation?

▶ What is the first thing you remember about the confrontation?

▶ What were you thinking about during the confrontation?

▶ How did that make you feel?

▶ Were you ever concerned for Mr. Defendant's safety?

▶ What, if anything, did you do in response to your concern about your Mr. Defendant's safety?

Ask your questions to draw responses that will appeal to the jury members' senses. For instance:

- ▶ What did that look like?
- ▶ What did that feel like?
- ▶ What did that sound like?
- ▶ You say you had blood in your mouth. What did that taste like?
- ▶ You said you could smell something burning. What did that smell like?

Descriptions of things in terms of the five senses help the jurors to remember and understand the facts better.

OBJECTIONS

Objections prevent the admission of improper evidence. They must be made immediately after the inappropriate question is posed or immediately after a witness makes an objectionable statement.

You should never go to trial without a good grasp of your jurisdiction's rules of evidence. If you do not know the rules of evidence, then you may miss objecting to irrelevant and prejudicial evidence that may help convict your client.

I am not going to reteach you the rules of evidence. However, under the federal rules of evidence, the following objections are common in criminal trials:

- ▶ The question is asking about irrelevant or inadmissible evidence: "Objection, relevance."
- ▶ The question is vague and ambiguous: "Objection, the question is vague and ambiguous, and therefore confusing."
- ▶ The question is compound: "Objection, the question is compound and confusing."
- ▶ The question has been previously asked and answered (which makes its answer cumulative and irrelevant): "Objection, asked and answered."
- ▶ The question lacks foundation : "Objection, lack of foundation."
- ▶ The question is outside of the scope of direct or cross-examination: "Objection, outside of the scope."
- ▶ The question calls for inadmissible character evidence: "Objection, the question calls for impermissible character evidence."
- ▶ The question lacks the necessary foundation: "Objection, lack of foundation."

- ▶ The witness lacks personal knowledge or experience to answer the question (lack of personal knowledge means the answer may call for speculation): "Objection, lack of personal knowledge."

- ▶ The question calls for the witness to guess or speculate: "Objection, calls for speculation."

- ▶ The question calls for an opinion that requires expertise that the witness lacks or it has not been established that the witness possesses: "Objection, calls for improper expert opinion."

- ▶ The examiner is arguing with the witness: "Objection, argumentative."

- ▶ The question calls for hearsay: "Objection, hearsay."

- ▶ The question improperly suggests the answer: "Objection, leading."

- ▶ The question misquotes the witness, misstates the evidence, or assumes facts not in evidence: "Objection, counsel is misstating the evidence" or "Objection, the question assumes facts not in evidence."

- ▶ The question calls for the witness to give a narrative account: "Objection, the question calls for a narrative."

- ▶ The witness has not properly responded to the question: "Objection, nonresponsive."

If the objection is sustained, the witness cannot answer the question or the attorney can move to strike the witness's response. But be careful when you ask the court to strike a response, because doing so often requires the court to restate the objectionable testimony, thereby allowing the jury to hear it twice. Sometimes, the best course is to leave it alone as you do not want the jury to hear the statement again.

Another hazard is that an attorney can object too much and annoy the jury. As with arguments and motions, pick your battles. If the question elicits a fact that you know will come in eventually, let the prosecution ask a leading question. Objecting to every objectionable thing causes the jury to think that the defense has something to hide.

JURY INSTRUCTION CONFERENCE

The court will normally take up the issue of jury instructions at the close of the evidence. However, the court will often demand that the parties submit proposed jury instructions before the beginning of the evidence so the court can review and revise them during the course of the trial.

Jury instructions consist of a group of instructions to the jury from the court, listing the law the jury must consider in deciding the defendant's guilt.

As discussed in Chapter 9, most jurisdictions have pattern instructions that are approved by a committee or the jurisdiction's highest court, and they are to be used in every case. Sometimes, a change of law will occur that is not reflected in the pattern instructions. In that event, both sides will craft a proposed instruction that reflects the new law.

Pay close attention to each instruction as cases are often won or lost based upon the wording of jury instructions.

If you believe that an instruction should be given or excluded, then you must make an argument to the court in support of giving or excluding the instruction. Failure to make a record of your objection waives the issue on appeal should the court overrule your argument.

I insist that each juror be provided his or her own set of instructions to read along with and to take back in the deliberation room. I do this because I was once told by a jury that was provided only one set of the instructions that the foreman of the jury kept the instructions and the jury relied upon his interpretation of them. It is much better to have 12 people interpreting the instructions than one person.

CLOSING ARGUMENT

Closing argument is an opportunity for each side to summarize the evidence and argue to the jury what the evidence means as to the defendant's guilt.

The prosecutor usually presents her argument first because she has the burden of proof. Often, she is allowed a brief rebuttal after the defense counsel is finished with his closing argument.

Most courts set time limits for closing argument. You can expect anywhere from 15 to 60 minutes. Often, the judge will give you a five-, two-, or one-minute warning when you are nearing the end of your time allotment.

If you have performed the necessary preparation in developing your trial strategy and theory of the case, closing argument should be the easiest part of the trial.

Consider the following when making your closing argument:

▶ *Begin with the theory of the case.* For example:

Ladies and gentleman, Joe Smith is not guilty. He could not have committed the crime. He was in another town, hours away. It is unclear from the prosecution's evidence who actually committed this crime.

▶ *Summarize the evidence and relate it to the law provided in the jury instructions.* The closing argument focuses upon the facts and evidence that support the theory of the case. If necessary, it discounts or explains those facts that are detrimental to the defense theory of the case. It is more factually specific and argumentative than the opening statement.

► *Closing argument do's and don'ts.*

▼ Do not begin opening by telling the jury that what you are about to tell them is not evidence.

▼ Do not begin with an apology for your behavior during the trial.

▼ Do not begin by thanking the jury for their service; go right into your argument, as time is of the essence. If you have time at the end, say, "I thank you for your time and attention."

▼ Begin with a bang. Begin your closing argument with a story, a statement, or a quote that catches the jurors' attention.

▼ Do not script the closing. Instead, make an outline that fits on a couple of pages. Scripting will only make you more nervous. This may cause you to rely too much on your script and begin to read your closing argument to the jury. Juries do not enjoy being read to. You need to mesmerize them and sell your theory of the case to them. No one is encouraged to buy something from a salesman who has to read his sales pitch. You may become flustered if you get off script. This can make the jury uncomfortable. This may make the jury feel that you are not confident in your theory of the case or that you do not believe in your theory of the case.

▼ Do not rehash or highlight the bad facts of the case.

▼ Do explain those bad facts that are unavoidably necessary to explain away in order for the jury to subscribe to the defense theory of the case.

▼ Do rely upon the wording of the jury instructions when making your arguments to the jury.

▼ If you feel it is necessary, review the burden of proof instruction and explain to the jury how it was not met. You may even wish to focus on the key elements, explaining how the prosecutor has failed to meet his burden of proof as to each element.

▼ As you become more experienced and confident in your trial skills, you should abandon arguing to the jury that the prosecutor has failed to meet his burden of proof. Contending that the prosecution has failed to meet its burden of proof can lead the jury to believe that you are arguing the defendant did it, but that the prosecutor did not prove it. Instead, you will argue that the defendant is innocent.

A sample Closing Argument Transcript is included as Exhibit PP on the enclosed CD-ROM. ❖

CHAPTER 10

Sentencing

Sentencing occurs after a plea of guilty or no contest has been entered, with or without a plea agreement, or following a judge or jury's verdict of guilty.

Often, sentencing does not occur immediately after the plea is accepted or verdict is rendered. In these cases, the court sets the matter over for a period of time in order for the parties and the court to prepare for sentencing.

Some jurisdictions require the defendant to undergo a presentencing evaluation, from which a report is prepared by court administration (usually the probation department) and given to the judge and the attorneys. This report may include the defendant's age, aliases, date of birth, Social Security number, a brief version of the facts surrounding the conviction, the defendant's criminal record, and the department's sentencing or probation recommendations. Although the judge is not required to follow its recommendations, this report usually has significant influence on sentencing.

A sample Presentence Investigation Report is included as Exhibit QQ on the enclosed CD-ROM. ➥

If given the opportunity at sentencing, always make an argument for the court to follow the plea agreement or to sentence the defendant to the lowest possible term (which may include incarceration, probation, or both).

FORMAT OF SENTENCING HEARING

During the sentencing hearing, it is the defense attorney's job to make argument and present any evidence that will help the court to decide the sentence against the defendant. This is true even if the parties have an agreement as to the exact sentence the defendant should receive, because the court is not a party to the plea agreement.

You do not need to make an opening statement; begin by asking the court for the sentence desired. For example: "Your Honor, I am asking that you place Mr. Smith on standard probation."

Since the defendant has the right of allocution (the right to present any evidence or argument to show why judgment should not be pronounced against him), the judge will often give the defense a choice whether to argue first or wait until after the prosecutor has made his argument.

If the judge asks you to present your argument first, and you desire to hear what the prosecutor has to say first, respectfully ask the court, "Your Honor, I would like to hear what the prosecutor has to say before I make my argument." I have never had a court deny this request. I find it best to present my argument last, as my issues are then fresher in the judge's mind.

Exhibit FF, the sample Transcript of Plea and Sentencing Hearing that was discussed in Chapter 7, also applies here. ➥

TIPS FOR SENTENCING PRESENTATION

1. *Follow the rules for addressing the court.* See "Tips for Making Oral Arguments in Open Court" listed in Chapter 6.

2. *Mitigate the facts of the crime of which your client was convicted.* Mitigation means to emphasize the favorable facts and minimize the bad facts against the defendant. For example, if the defendant is being sentenced for the crime of aggravated robbery, stress to the court that the defendant was not the one who pulled the gun on the store clerk, but that he merely drove the getaway car. In some judges' minds, waving a gun at a person is more heinous than driving the gunman away from the scene.

3. *Present the defendant's accomplishments and disabilities.* As with negotiating a plea with the prosecutor, it is important to let the judge know about the defendant's good character and any disabilities that may make him a better candidate for probation. Expanding on the examples mentioned in Chapter 7, Plea Agreement:

   ▼ A defendant's military service may tell the judge that the defendant can be a productive member of society and that he can complete tasks he is assigned, which may help persuade the judge that the defendant can successfully complete probation conditions.

   ▼ A college degree may also tell the judge that the defendant can be a productive member of society and can complete assigned tasks; thus, he is amenable to probation.

   ▼ Being the sole support of four children is important because no judge enjoys making children wards of the state. The judge may place the defendant on probation instead of sending him to jail.

- ▼ Unemployment may tell the judge that this was a one-time mistake, that defendant committed the crime because he needed the money. Thus, the court may be lenient on sentencing.

- ▼ If the defendant checked himself into substance abuse or anger management treatment as a result of the arrest, the judge may believe that the defendant is taking responsibility for his actions and serious about straightening out his life.

- ▼ Schizophrenia may be an excuse for the defendant's actions (even if the defendant refused to run an insanity defense or failed in doing so).

- ▼ A serious physical illness such as stage 2 lymphoma is relevant because no judge wants to incarcerate a person suffering from cancer or require the state to pay for the defendant's medical treatment.

4. *Present physical proof to the court substantiating defendant's accomplishments or disabilities.* Any physical proof that substantiates your claims of defendant's accomplishments or disabilities will help the court understand them. The court may be suspicious of your claims without something to substantiate them. Have copies of military discharge papers, college diplomas, unemployment check stubs, and medical records; show photographs of the children; produce prescription bottles.

5. *Prepare your client to speak to the court.* The defendant has the right of allocution, that is, the right to speak on his own behalf to the judge and make a plea for mercy. Ordinarily, it is the client's own words that matter to the court when the decision is made to be lenient.

   Depending on the client, I sometimes advise the client not to say a word or to limit what is said to something like, "I am sorry for what I have done, and I want to prove to the court that this will not happen again." I do this because every word spoken by the defendant to the judge is highly scrutinized and can be misinterpreted and used against him when the sentence is being handed down. Even the defendant's body language while making his statement can be misinterpreted and used against him.

   You cannot, however, keep the client from speaking. It is his right to make a statement on his behalf at sentencing. The following points are helpful to assist the client with his statement to the court:

   - ▼ Ask the defendant to write out ahead of time what he desires to say.

   - ▼ Suggest that the defendant take responsibility for her actions, if she is able to (If she maintained her innocence through a trial, you may not want her to take any responsibility in the event that the matter is overturned on appeal and retried.)

▼ Advise the defendant to avoid making statements blaming others or criticizing the court, the prosecutor, law enforcement involved in the case, or evidence involved in the case.

▼ Read and edit the speech.

6. *Keep the defendant's minor children out of the courtroom.* Advise your client and his family to leave minor children at home at the time of sentencing. Children do not bring sympathy to the defendant. They make judges feel like they are being manipulated. If the children appear despite your advice, make the family take them out of the courtroom, and preferably, out of the courthouse.

CHALLENGING THE CRIMINAL HISTORY OR THE PRESENTENCING EVALUATION REPORT

It is often appropriate to challenge the assertions made in the presentencing evaluation report and the defendant's criminal history set out in this report or presented by the prosecutor.

Presentencing reports are often prepared by probation officers or other courthouse employees and they can be very biased against the defendant. They can distort the facts of the case or the defendant's criminal history. The criminal history that is contained in these reports or presented by the prosecutor is often taken from a law enforcement database (e.g., NCIC) without any verifications of the convictions contained in the history.

If you disagree with the allegations made by these reports or the prosecutor you should file a motion challenging them or advise the judge in open court that you challenge the same and request that the judge either ignore the assertions for lack of proof or require that the prosecutor prove the claims being made. Often, the prosecution has the burden to prove the defendant's criminal history by a preponderance of the evidence or by clear and convincing evidence if the defense challenges the criminal history presented.

Review the statute regarding this issue because some jurisdictions have a rule of law that the defendant waives the right to challenge his criminal history in the future if he does not challenge it upon the first opportunity to do so.

A sample Motion to Challenge Criminal History is included as Exhibit RR on the enclosed CD-ROM. ➥

DEALING WITH VICTIM IMPACT STATEMENTS

Most jurisdictions allow the victim or anyone harmed by the defendant's crime to make a statement to the judge at sentencing. In my experience, these statements tend to criticize the defendant and the criminal justice system. Some ask for wildly disproportionate penalties (e.g., to have the defendant put to death or castrated).

Warn the defendant of the potential for such statements before the proceeding and tell him to keep his head down and his mouth shut. The judge secretly watches the defendant while these statements are being made and judges the defendant according to his reaction to the same.

I once saw a judge refuse to follow the plea agreement and sentence the defendant to the maximum potential sentence, having found the defendant to be remorseless. The judge claimed that he watched the defendant glare at the victim while she read her victim impact statement to the court.

A sample Victim Impact Statement is included as Exhibit SS on the enclosed CD-ROM. ➙

Index

U
upward departure sentences, 20
U.S. Constitution
  14th Amendment, 31
  Fourth Amendment, 39
  Sixth Amendment, 31

V
venue, motion to change, 73
victim impact statements, 141
voir dire, 117–123

W
waivers, of preliminary hearings,
  51–53
warrants
  motion to suppress and, 77–78
  for searches, 39–40

"with intent," defined, 21
witnesses
  for alibi, 36, 44, 74
  controlling, 127–128
  cross-examining, 49–51, 110–111,
    126–129
  defendant as, 130
  direct examination of, 129–132
  interviewing, 100–101
  missing, 52
  preparing list of, 115
  tampering with, 34
*World's Best Anatomical Charts,
  The* (Anatomical Chart
  Co.), 98